Joe Geraghty is a founding member of Vision Sports Ireland. As an athlete he won eight Irish national track titles as well as winning three UK National gold medals between 1981 and 1985. In 1983 he won silver at 5000m at the IBSA European Games in Bulgaria and subsequently represented Ireland at the 1984 Paralympic Games in the USA. Off track, Joe has dedicated his life to supporting the work of Vision Sports Ireland, serving in numerous roles over five decades and becoming president in 2024.

Liz

A wonderful lady to chat with as Katie, my baby celebrate her wedding Take care of yourself
Joe Geraghty

Out of Sight!

**Stories of Ireland's
Blind and Vision Impaired
Sportspeople**

OUT OF SIGHT!

Stories of Ireland's Blind and Vision Impaired Sportspeople

JOE GERAGHTY

MARTELLO

**OUT OF SIGHT! STORIES OF IRELAND'S
BLIND AND VISION IMPAIRED SPORTSPEOPLE**

First published in 2024 by
Martello Publishing
Glenshesk House
10 Richview Office Park
Clonskeagh
Dublin D14 V8C4
Republic of Ireland
www.martellopublishing.ie

Copyright © Joe Geraghty, 2024
The right of Joe Geraghty to be identified as the author of this work has been asserted in accordance with the provisions of the Copyright and Related Rights Act, 2000.

All rights reserved. No part of this publication may be reproduced in any form or by any means without the prior permission of the author.

A CIP catalogue record for this book is available from the British Library

Print ISBN: 978-1-7396086-5-1
Ebook ISBN: 978-1-7396086-6-8
Martello Publishing gratefully acknowledges the financial support of Vision Ireland Foundation, Kildare County Council and the Granville Hotel, Waterford.

Printed by Opolgraf SA, Opole, Poland
Typesetting and design by Niall McCormack
Typeset in Dashiell Text and Field Gothic
10 9 8 7 6 5 4 3 2 1

Dedicated to the ones I love:
my wife Grainne and my children,
Claire, Chris, Ellie and Katie

Author's note on terminology

'b/vi' is an abbreviation to indicate 'blind/vision impaired'. The abbreviation will be used extensively in this book.

Historically, a variety of terms have been used to describe blindness and its various levels. Terms have included sight loss, the blind, low vision, visually or vision impaired, partially sighted, black blind and sightless and a few more which are unprintable!

Most people now interpret 'blind' to describe those with no sight and 'vision impaired' in relation to those with limited vision.

Blind/vision impaired – many replace the '/' with an 'and' or 'or' – is about the most acceptable term right now so, let's go with it.

Contents

    Timeline: Rolling back the years   17

    Introduction: I gotta get a message to you – Jason Smyth   23

1. **Get back** – *Get back to where you once belonged – our century of change.*   27

2. **River deep mountain high** – *Paula Dorrington and Gus Dorrington (Dublin), including athletics, mountain climbing and skiing.*   31

3. **In the summertime** – *With summer campers Annie Donnelly (Tipperary), Catherine Walsh (Dublin), Tony Lyster (Dublin), Carol Carr (Dublin), Grainne Geraghty (Kildare), Jacqui McKeating (Dublin/UK), Margaret Hughes (Kildare) Breda Currid (Dublin) and Róisín Dermody (Carlow).*   35

4. **Heroes** – *Two centuries ago.*   40

5. **The games people play** – *A century ago. Early competitions in athletics, cricket, Gaelic games, rowing, skittles and swimming.*   43

6. **This used to be my playground** – *School for blind boys with Des Kenny (Kildare) and Philip Doyle (Mayo) including basketball, board games, crab football, cricket, paper ball, swimming and trolley racing.*   47

7. **In a lifetime** – *Athletes Jim Gallagher (Mayo) and Michael Delaney (Dublin), including tandem cycling, marathons and track and field.*   51

8. **School's out** – *School for blind girls with Sr Brid (Clare), Carol Carr (Dublin), Catherine Walsh (Dublin) and Katie-George Dunlevy (Donegal/UK) including athletics, rounders and swimming.*   54

9. **Top of the world** – *Para-cyclist Katie-George Dunlevy (Donegal/UK), including downhill skiing, para-rowing, swimming and tandem cycling.*   58

10. **To see or not to see** – *Vision-impaired classes with Paralympics Ireland classification manager Ana Maia (Brazil/Ireland).*   63

11. **Jump!** – *My early days.*   67

12. **The letter** – *Where national organised sport began, with Martin Kelly (Kildare), featuring athletics.*   70

13. **Hey Frankie** – *Swim coach Frank Cullinan (Dublin).*   74

14. **Here, there, and almost everywhere** – *Spreading the word with Gerry Campbell (Longford), Anne Kelly, née McKay (Scotland/Kildare) and Des Kenny (Kildare). The early days of national organised sport for b/vi people.*   78

15. **The wind beneath our wings** – *Pat Kelly (Louth/Limerick), including athletics and tandem cycling*   82

16. **Money's too tight to mention** – *Fundraising frolics featuring Gay Byrne, Eamonn Coghlan and Eamon Dunphy.*   86

17. **I only want to tee with you** – *Ian Corr (Dublin) and Jimmy Murray (Kilkenny), featuring blind golf.*   92

18. **My mama always told me there'd be mays like this** – *May Games/Mayfest 1981 – present.*   96

19. **Gold** – *Athlete Carol Carr (Dublin).* 100

20. **I get a kick out of you** – *Futsal with player/coach Tony Lyster (Dublin) and vi rugby captain Sean McDowell (Down). Gaelic games also included.* 103

21. **Hanging on the telephone** – *The founding of Vision Sports Ireland.* 108

22. **I will walk 500 miles** – *Walking and trekking with Theresa Lavin (Meath) and Michael Lavin (Roscommon).* 112

23. **Ride on** – *Equine therapy with ChildVision occupational therapy manager Audrey Darby (Dublin).* 116

24. **Simply the best** – *Athlete Bridie Lynch (Donegal).* 121

25. **Here comes the knight** – *Braille chess with Philip Doyle (Mayo).* 125

26. **You've got a friend in me** – *Tony Guest (Louth) and John Newman (Longford), featuring road running.* 129

27. **Off the wall** – *What goes on outside the village.* 134

28. **Wheelin' in the years** – *Tandem cycling.* 137

29. **Don't stop believin'** – *Rahim Nazarali (Dublin/Kenya), featuring judo.* 142

30. **Against all odds** – *Hosting 1993 European Athletics Championships, Dublin, with Mick McKeon (Wexford), Ann Lyster (Monaghan) and Tony Lyster (Dublin).* 146

31. **Two outta three ain't bad** – *Catherine Walsh (Dublin), including para-athletics, para-triathlon and tandem cycling.* 151

32. **We are family** – *With Joe Walsh and Bernie Walsh (Dublin), the Cusack family (Waterford) and Bernie Everard (Kildare).* 156

33. **Annie's song** – *Kathleen Donnelly with daughter Annie Donnelly (Tipperary), including swimming and tandem cycling.*
   160

34. **Our eyes adored you** – *Prof. Michael O'Keeffe, President, Vision Sports Ireland 2015-23.* 164

35. **Girls' talk** – *Women in sport including Greta Streimikyte (Dublin/Lithuania), Orla Comerford (Dublin), Babs Weiberg (Louth/Germany), Sinead Kane (Cork), Hilary Devlin (Dublin) and Róisín Dermody (Carlow).* 168

36. **Knock, knock, knockin' on Kevin's door** – *Blind football with player Kevin Kelly (Donegal) and manager Alex Whelan (Dublin).* 173

37. **With a little help from our friends** – *Volunteers, guides, pilots, drivers.* 178

38. **Fields of gold** – *Multi-sport with Wally Roode (Dublin/South Africa), including athletics, blind golf, cricket, para-triathlon, parkrun, rugby and wrestling.* 185

39. **Let's hear it for the boys** – *Men in sport, including Fintan O'Donnell (Limerick), Conal McNamara (Mayo), Mick Clarke (Meath), James Brown (Down), Donnacha McCarthy (Cork) and Tony Ward (Monaghan).* 189

40. **What's another steer** – *Rally navigator Sara McFadden (Mayo), including camogie and rally navigation.* 194

41. **New York state of mind** – *Blind golfer Paul McCormack (Donegal/USA).* 198

42. **No matter how I tri** – *With para-triathlete Chloe MacCombe (Derry) and Eamonn Tilley (Dublin).* 202

43. **Love is all around** – *Vi tennis with manager Liam O'Donohoe (Wexford) and player Babs Weiberg (Louth/Germany).* 207

44. **Marguerite time** – *Vi tennis player Marguerite Quinn (Limerick).* 211

45. **The boat that I row** – *Water sports with Shane Ryan (Limerick), Michael Lavin (Roscommon), Hilary Devlin (Dublin) and Rahim Nazarali (Dublin/Kenya), including kayaking, rowing, sailing and water-skiing.* 215

46. **Take it to the limit** – *Zero limits at Mondello with Aaron Mullaniff, CEO, Vision Sports Ireland, and Sara McFadden (Mayo). B/vi people drive dual-controlled cars.* 219

47. **Waterfront** – *Swimmer Róisín Ní Riain (Limerick).* 224

48. **Brand-new key** – *Release from Covid-19 lockdown with Aaron Mullaniff and Pádraig Healy, National Sports Development Manager, Vision Sports Ireland.* 228

49. **Here comes tomorrow** – *The next phase.* 233

50. **After the gold rush** – *Jason Smyth MBE.* 239

Acknowledgements 247

Your contacts: support organisations for blind and vision-impaired people in Ireland 250

Timeline:
Rolling back the years

- **1831:** The Ulster Society – an education centre supporting deaf and blind children – was founded in Belfast. In 1961 the school moved to Jordanstown, Antrim.

- **1832:** The Perkins School for the Blind was founded by Dr Samuel Gridley Howe in Boston, Massachusetts. At this world-leading school, Howe developed the first comprehensive fitness programme for blind/vision-impaired (b/vi) children incorporating early-morning sea-swimming and running.

- **1858:** St Mary's Blind Asylum for Roman Catholic Females was founded in Merrion, Dublin, by the Catholic Sisters of Charity. It closed in 2001.

- **1858:** St Joseph's Asylum for Roman Catholic boys was founded in Drumcondra, Dublin by the Catholic Carmelite Order. They managed the complex until 1955, when the Catholic Rosminian Order took charge. Its primary school was officially recognised by the Department of Education in 1960.

- **1868:** The Royal National Institute for the Blind (RNIB) was founded by Dr Thomas Rhodes Armitage. Its initial name was the British and Foreign Society for Improving the Embossed Literature of the Blind.

- **1868:** Worcester College for the Blind Sons of Gentlemen was founded by Church of England clergymen. The school sports syllabus was extensive and innovative.

- **1871:** The Royal Normal College for the Blind, now the Royal National College for the Blind (RNC), was founded by Dr Thomas Rhodes Armitage and Frances Joseph Campbell in Crystal Palace, London. Campbell was recognised as the world's leading educator for b/vi children. He founded the 'Playground Movement' – sport for fun – and built an accessible gym, skating rinks, swimming pools and one of the largest playgrounds in the British Isles.

- **1899:** The National League of the Blind of Ireland (NLBI) was founded in Dublin.

- **1931:** The National Council for the Blind of Ireland (NCBI), now Vision Ireland, was founded by Alice Stanley Armitage in Dublin. Alice is daughter of Dr. Thomas Rhodes Armitage, founder of the RNIB.

- **1948:** The Stoke Mandeville Games – for disabled World War II veterans – were held. The brainchild of Dr Ludwig Guttmann, the Stoke Mandeville event is now generally accepted as the Games which lit the torch and led us to the modern Paralympic movement.

- **1960:** Inaugural Paralympic Games were held in Rome, Italy.

- **1961:** Inaugural Braille Chess Olympiad was held in Meschede, West Germany.

- **1964:** Ireland competed at the 2nd Braille Chess Olympiad, Bad Kühlungsborn, East Germany.

- **1976:** Goalball was introduced as first b/vi competitive sport at the 5th Paralympic Games, Toronto, Canada. Four years earlier the sport was demonstrated at the Heidelberg, West Germany, Paralympic Games.

- **1976:** Irish Guide Dogs was founded.

- **1976:** British Blind Sports (BBS) was founded to support access to sport for b/vi people in Great Britain and Northern Ireland.

- **1978:** Jim Sherwin, presenter of RTÉ Radio's *Listen and See*, read a letter from Anne McKay, inviting listeners to attend inaugural UK Athletics Championships for the Blind in Grangemouth Scotland. Six Irish athletes attend.

- **1979:** The first Sports Club for the Blind in Ireland was founded.

- **1979:** The Sports Club joined the National League of the Blind of Ireland and became known as the Sports and Social Club of the National League of the Blind.

- **1980:** The Irish Wheelchair Association (IWA) Sport invited two Irish blind and vision-impaired athletes – Martin and Pat Kelly – to represent Ireland at the 6th Paralympic Games in Arnhem, Netherlands.

- **1981:** Inaugural Mayfest held in Dublin, supported by NLBI and the Department of Education (Sport).

- **1981:** The Ireland team competed at the first European Games for the Blind, Fulda, West Germany. Carol Carr took home our first gold medals, in athletics.

- **1981:** The International Blind Federation (IBSA) was founded in Paris.

- **1983:** Fighting Blindness Ireland founded.

- **1984:** In New York, USA, Carol Carr became Ireland's first b/vi athlete to win gold at the 7th Paralympic Games. Her event: B2 400m.

- **1986:** Charles J. Haughey, three times Taoiseach, attended Mayfest.

- **1988:** Vision Sports Ireland, then Irish Blind Sports, was founded in Dublin.

- **1989:** The International Paralympic Committee (IPC) was founded in Dusseldorf, West Germany.

- **1992:** Féach, the Republic of Ireland support charity for parents of b/vi children, was founded.

- **1993:** Ireland hosted the 7th European Athletics Championships in Dublin. President Mary Robinson and Taoiseach Albert Reynolds attend ed as 300 athletes competed.

- **1996:** In Atlanta, USA, Bridie Lynch became Ireland's second b/vi athlete to win gold at the Paralympic Games. Her event: F3 Discus.

- **2005:** Two unannounced athletes attended the 25th Anniversary Mayfest in Dublin. They both attained the required standards and qualified to make their debuts at para-sport: Michael McKillop and Jason Smyth soon become Ireland's most successful disabled athletes, winning multiple gold medals and smashing several world records.

- **2007:** Angel Eyes, the Northern Ireland support charity for parents of b/vi children, was founded.

- **2008:** In Beijing, China, Jason Smyth won double gold at the Paralympic Games. His events: T13 100m and T13 200m.

- **2012:** In London, Jason Smyth won double gold at the Paralympic Games. His events: T13 100m and T13 200m.

- **2013:** Irish Blind Sports re-branded to Vision Sports Ireland.

- **2016:** Michael D. Higgins, President of Ireland, attended Mayfest in Dublin.

- **2016:** In Rio de Janeiro, Brazil, Katie-George Dunlevy (stoker) and Eve McCrystal (pilot) won Ireland's first tandem cycling gold at the Paralympic Games. Their event: B Tandem Road Time Trial.

- **2016:** Jason Smyth won gold at Paralympic Games. His event: T13 100m. Note: organisers dropped T13 200m.

- **2018:** Ireland hosted the 2nd World Tennis Championships for b/vi players. The event was held at Shankill Lawn Tennis Club, Co. Dublin.

- **2019:** Ireland hosted the 4th Vision Cup, the Ryder Cup of Blind Golf at Portmarnock Golf Links, Co. Dublin.

- **2020:** Vision Sports Ireland merged with NCBI (now Vision Ireland) as a subsidiary not-for-profit body and registered charity.

- **2021:** The 40th anniversary Mayfest saw the return of participants and officials from all previous May games as they hosted a Covid-induced virtual opening ceremony. The virtual closing ceremony was hosted by RTÉ's Miriam O'Callaghan with guest speaker 1984 Olympic Marathon silver medallist John Treacy.

- In Tokyo, Japan, Katie-George Dunlevy and Eve McCrystal won double gold at the Paralympic Games. Their events: B Tandem Time Trial and Road Race.

- Jason Smyth won gold at the Paralympic Games. His event: T13 100m.

Introduction:
I gotta get a message to you

Jason Smyth MBE

In the world of sport we think of triumphs, challenges and the unbreakable determination that creates stories inspiring and resonating with people across the globe. But what about the lesser-told tales, the extraordinary journeys of those who navigate the world of sport without the gift of sight?

It is my great honour and privilege to introduce *Out of Sight!*, authored by my trusted friend Joe Geraghty. Joe takes us on an intriguing journey, shedding light on the lives of blind and vision-impaired sportspeople in Ireland. For the first time ever, this book unveils the rich history of sports for blind and vision-impaired individuals, providing a whistlestop tour through the various sporting realms as recounted by the players, their families, friends and coaches.

Through sixty compelling interviews conducted by Joe, the captivating narratives come to life, painting a vivid portrait of dedication, resilience and the pursuit of greatness. We encounter a vast array of sports, exploring the depths of over forty disciplines. From the echoing cheers in the athletics stadium to the rhythmic swish of a judo throw, each chapter reveals insights from these individuals.

Joe, a person wholeheartedly devoted to the Vision Sports movement since its inception five decades ago, leads us on this fascinating journey with enthusiasm and first-hand knowledge.

But who is Joe Geraghty, the driving force behind this book?

His connection to the world of blind and vision-impaired sports runs deep, as demonstrated by his own achievements and contributions as a visually impaired athlete. In 1981 Joe won the first-ever athletics race at the inaugural May Games, now known as Mayfest, in the 1500m. Just three years later, he went on to proudly represent Ireland at the 1984 Paralympic Games in the USA.

I first met Joe in 2005. I was marking my first step into para-sport at Mayfest, as I competed in the 100m, and that is where my successful journey on the track began. Three years later I competed in my first Paralympic Games in Beijing, where I won double gold in the 100m and 200m.

Joe Geraghty's contributions to the sports community in Ireland extend far beyond his time as an athlete. He spent many years as a sports administrator, serving as the chairperson at Vision Sports Ireland, where I had the opportunity to work with him and witness the indelible mark he left on the organisation's growth.

Moreover, Joe's diverse experiences extend beyond the sports realm, as he held a senior role as a government IT database administrator. Before joining the civil service, he wrote many articles for Ireland's No. 1 showbiz magazine of yesteryear, *New Spotlight*. Later, he edited *Public Service News* as well as the sports pages of *Public Sector Times*. His passion and dedication to sports for people with visual impairments make him the ideal guide to unravel the stories that lie within the pages of *Out of Sight!*.

Together, let us celebrate the triumphs, embrace the challenges, and explore the extraordinary lives of blind and vision-impaired sportspeople in Ireland.

Jason Smyth MBE

1. **Get back**

Get back to where you once belonged – our century of change.

Jimmy, Paddy, and Johnny kick off a game of football on their local village green. School's out as the brothers enjoy a few weeks away from lockup in St Joseph's School for Blind Boys (JoJo's), which they called 'The Drum' because of its Drumcondra, Dublin location.

It's 1930s Ireland, and the midlands townspeople of Kilbeggan go shopping or to church. Some may clock in for work at the nearby whiskey distillery, while others may prefer to have it 'distilled' to them at the local pub.

The footballing siblings – all have hereditary eye conditions with resulting partial sight – are having fun.

Two local gardaí pedal up and shout at the boys, 'Go home, you're not allowed out! If *yis* don't go home, we'll send you back to your asylum in Dublin!'

Game over.

Fifty years later, the middle sibling, Paddy, was in Long Island, New York, where he saw his son – that's me – walk with the Irish team at the Opening Ceremony of the 7th Paralympic Games. On 19 June 1984, 9,000 members of the NYPD and US security services were on hand as President Ronald Reagan welcomed the 3,000-plus participants.

No chance Paddy could be sent back to the asylum now. He was treated like a king by the NYPD, who ensured he was well fed and watered.

Paddy, his siblings and his contemporaries came a long way in half a century: from not being allowed to play sports in the open to their offspring competing on the world stage.

In the past five decades, organised sport – local, national, and international – for b/vi people in Ireland has developed at a rapid pace. However, public perception and awareness have lagged for much of this time as people try their best to understand the abilities of people with disabilities. It was always going to be a slow bicycle race; it still is.

The pace of awareness picked up over a decade ago. The London 2012 Paralympics was a game-changer. Great Britain, Ireland and the world packed out all venues for every single event, unlike preceding Paralympics, where you could hear your echo in the empty stadia.

The mass media were in overdrive. We had live TV beaming, social media streaming and newspapers screaming headlines of major Paralympic achievements.

Ireland's Jason Smyth, who has less than 10 per cent vision, grabbed all the headlines.

In the late summer of 2012, lightning Smyth struck twice, emulating Usain Bolt by striking double sprint gold at the London Stadium. Curiously, Smyth, the undefeated sprint champion of the para-sport world, thought he may have been overtaken in the heats of the London 100m. He wasn't, and the full story will emerge later in this book.

Trailblazer Jason Smyth holds twenty-one Paralympic, World and European gold medals. His influence and impact in the world of disabled and b/vi people is incalculable.

Partially sighted cyclist Katie-George Dunlevy is fast catching Smyth with twelve international championship golds, including three at the Paralympic Games. Carol Carr was first to the streets of gold when winning at 1500m at the 1981 European Championships in West Germany. Her final gold tally was five, including victory at the 1984 Paralympic Games. Bridie Lynch brought home Ireland's sole gold at Atlanta 1996 to add to her European gold ten years earlier. Para-cyclist Catherine Walsh won World gold in Los Angeles 2012 and European 800m athletics gold eleven years earlier.

Limerick's Róisín Ní Riain won World Championship gold in Paris in 2023 and went on to win two European golds a year later. Her teammate Greta Streimikyte is a two-time European champion. If you're counting, Ireland's b/vi competitors have won an astonishing forty-six gold medals to date at international para-sport championships.

Since our debut in 1980, thirty-eight b/vi people have represented Ireland at Paralympic Games in athletics, tandem cycling, judo, rowing, swimming, para-triathlon and equestrian.

But, beyond the ups and downs of the Paralympics, there are the highs of the 99.5 per cent of b/vi sportspeople who enjoy the great outdoors and indoors. Like everyone else, they do it for health, fitness, well-being and fun. In addition, b/vi people feel sport minimises isolation and helps with that extra confidence required to get out and about. Those with very low or no vision say it helps build spatial awareness.

There's scope for many more people in Ireland with all levels of blindness to play the game.

According to Census 2022, 296,601 people are living in Ireland who experience blindness or a vision impairment. 65,099 reported difficulties in going outside the home (21.9 per cent), while 76,884 reported difficulties participating in other activities (25.9 per cent).

2023 research conducted by DCU in association with Vision Sports Ireland and Vision Ireland found 'physical activity levels (among b/vi people) were low, with only 21.7% achieving World Health Organisation (WHO) guidelines of 30 minutes of moderate to vigorous physical levels five days a week. These figures are significantly lower than a comparison study of the general population at 41%.' (Sport Ireland, 2021).

Most of these statistics are new, with no back comparison. However, we can be sure we have taken massive strides, particularly in recent decades.

Much done, much more to be done.

2. River deep mountain high

*Paula Dorrington and Gus Dorrington (Dublin),
including athletics, mountain climbing and skiing.*

'I'm still alive because of sport,' Paula Dorrington tells me three times during my lunchtime visit to her home. 'I've been a diabetic since I was nine, which resulted in me losing my eyesight. At twenty-three, I became epileptic.'

Paula recalls finding sport – and love – at her new job at Blindcraft in the early 80s. Irish Blindcraft, closed now for two decades, was the state agency that provided employment for b/vi people in skills such as basketry.

Paula says, 'One of the girls told me about Gus, who was working facing me all the time. He was a runner, she said, who trained with a gang of b/vi athletes each Saturday. A few weeks later, Gus asked me to join him at a session. I agreed but didn't think I was going to run, as I was diabetic and overweight. After a few exercises, I was wrecked, but coach Tony Guest kept with me. When it was over, Tony asked me back the following week, and I thought, no chance!

'Then I checked my glucose meter, and I couldn't believe it – my blood sugar had gone down quite a bit.

'Back at work on Monday, Gus asked if I enjoyed the Saturday session. I told him I loved it! Gus offered to take me running midweek. He ran the eight-mile round trip across Dublin to my home and back. We used a string to link us.'

Paula and Gus were soon tethered together in every sense and tied the knot in matrimony in 1997.

In a b/vi person's world, the one-eye guy is king. So, Gus, with his limited vision, had sufficient sight to assist Paula. Gus is from a one-child family, and he was born twelve weeks premature in 1959. 'I was a miracle baby,' says Gus. 'Babies weren't born under thirty weeks back then.'

'My eye condition is retinopathy of prematurity (ROP), an eye disorder caused by abnormal blood vessels throughout the retina. There was too much oxygen in the incubator. (To see a full list of sight conditions with explanations visit the website fightingblindness.ie/living-with-sight-loss/eye-conditions/.)

'My parents didn't realise how bad my sight was, so I attended mainstream school at Dublin's Synge Street, with fifty-two pupils in my class. One of the teachers there told my mum about St Joseph's, where they specialised in children with poor sight and where there were smaller classes. I moved at age twelve and never looked back. I played all the sports and games there, from crab football to chess.'

Gus learned the skills of basketry at St Joseph's. Ten years later, he returned there as a paid part-time instructor.

Gus always sees the funny side of running blind. 'I was jogging along the River Liffey before one of our Saturday sessions,' he recalls. 'I saw a guy on a bike coming at me. He was a canoeing coach yelling instructions to his crews. I moved to the water's edge to allow him to pass. He also goes to the edge, jams on his breaks, and goes head over handlebars into the water. His crews cheered in delight!

Paula remembers a day she and Gus were jogging along the canal tethered using string: 'This eight- or nine-year-old kid calls over to Gus, "That's the way to have her, Mister, on the lead!"'

Meanwhile, by the mid-80s, Paula's health and fitness had improved in leaps and bounds, and soon she was setting Irish b/vi sprint records. Gus and Paula travelled around the Great Britain and Irish b/vi athletics circuit from Dublin to Birmingham, and London to Manchester. Paula collected medals at sprints, javelin and shot-put, while Gus picked up his accolades at distances from 100m to 800m.

Paula's family are steeped in sport. Her brother, footballer Brian Duff, was a member of the star-studded Liverpool soccer squad of the late 70s. On returning home, he won five trophies in Ireland, including the League and FAI Cup with Dundalk.

Back in Ireland, while Gus and Paula were competing across the UK, I was engaged in athletics management, formulating qualifying standards for our teams competing in European, World and Paralympic Championships. My involvement with this process precluded me from qualification, which was never an issue for me.

Gus says, 'The change to qualifying standards was good news for me, as I think the old selection process worked against me.'

Both Gus and Paula achieved the standards for the 1988 Seoul Paralympic Games. Gus ran excellent times in the 400m and 800m. Despite a lane mix-up at 100m, Paula attained top results in the javelin and shot-put.

Paula recalls, 'It was our first big competition, and we both performed to our best. The city of Seoul was wonderful, but there was incredible poverty in the areas around the Paralympic Village. There were mothers with babies queuing outside the Paralympic Village long before the Games had finished. They were waiting to take possession of our accommodation as their new homes once we had departed.' Paula won her first major championship medals in javelin at the European Championships in Caen, France, in 1991. A year later, she returned to Paralympic Games. At Barcelona 92, she competed in five events, achieving top-10 finishes in the 100m, 200m, long jump, javelin and shot-put. Injury and hospitalisation ruled Gus out of Barcelona.

Paula is no stranger to hospitals, either. 'But sport still saves my health,' she comments. 'Sport means everything, both physically and mentally. I've also met so many people and travelled the world.'

Gus recalls meeting the late football legend Bobby Charlton at the 1984 Manchester Games.

'Sport was so good to Paula and me,' says Gus. 'Paula tandem-cycled – bicycle-for-two where the fully-sighted person pilots while the b/vi cyclist pedals like hell – across Australia, and we both skied in Europe and trekked to base camp at Everest. Two years later, I returned to the Himalayas and climbed Mera Peak, over 21,000 feet above sea level.'

Back to earth now, and two very excited guide dogs put an end to lunch with Gus and Paula: Diva, Gus's guide, and Tessa, Paula's dog, demanded their afternoon walk.

I couldn't win here. I was licked.

3. In the summertime

With summer campers Annie Donnelly (Tipperary), Catherine Walsh (Dublin), Tony Lyster (Dublin), Carol Carr (Dublin), Grainne Geraghty (Kildare), Jacqui McKeating (Dublin/UK), Margaret Hughes (Kildare), Breda Currid (Dublin), and Róisín Dermody (Carlow).

Summer nights dancing in the Fermanagh moonlight, summer days kayaking in Kerry. Some made it to the green fields of France, others to the Austrian, Italian and Swiss lakes.

For over half a century, b/vi children and some adults have enjoyed summer and Easter camps and inter-school and club tours.

Margaret Hughes (*née* Hennessey) recalls in her teenage years excitedly collecting coins and running down to the red phone box at St Mary's, Merrion, to call Arthur Mitchell MBE. Arthur had just been on *Listen and See* on RTÉ Radio promoting 'Derrygiff Activities for the Blind'.

Arthur had places available for a cross-community summer camp in Lough Erne, Co. Fermanagh. The camps were run over a fortnight, with fifteen b/vi adults from both sides of the Irish border participating for one week. A similar number of teens participated during the alternate week.

Host Arthur, who lost his sight in his early twenties, ran the Derrygiff charity to help b/vi people build confidence to take on life's challenges.

I Zoomed with Margaret and her lifelong friends Carol Carr, Grainne Geraghty (née McGlone), Jacqui McKeating (née Fulham), and Breda Currid (née Moran).

For thirty minutes the girls laughed their way through their Derrygiff memories from 1981 onwards. Margaret told her dad she was off to Cavan as he wouldn't let her cross the border because of the Troubles. Grainne told her dad she'd be sleeping in a field with no phone contact.

With no rain gear, the girls got washed out of it and recall one major bomb scare. Unbothered, they sang and danced the nights away by the campfire or at the local disco.

By day, the girls were in and out of the water at duck's speed. They went canoeing, water-skiing, caving, walking, kayaking, zip wiring and abseiling. They remember intense training before participating in activities with support from the RUC (now PSNI) and the British army.

Paralympic star Catherine Walsh joined the northern summer camps a decade later. 'In 1990, I took part in a cross-border ski trip to Bulgaria, associated with the Mitchells. I then joined their summer camp where I tried so many sports, which I otherwise would never have done. Abseiling, potholing and swimming through caves. I love caves to this day.'

Like Catherine, multi-sports queen Róisín Dermody met the Mitchells through skiing and then landed to earth not in Enniskillen but in north Yorkshire. The Irish cross-border troupe were on tour. It wasn't quite a once-off meet-up for Róisín, who recalls, 'Yeah, during lockdown on social media, I ended up chatting with two guys from Northern Ireland who I met thirty years ago through those Mitchell trips.'

Ann and Tony Lyster, two lynchpins of the early Vision Sports days, have fond memories of cross-border camps in the

90s involving angling, water sports and tenpin bowling. Their favourite memory was at Kilancrott in Cavan.

Tony comments, 'We climbed up a steep hill to do a 40-foot jump into a pond. I was scared, but jumping was easier than climbing back down again.

'It's a pity we don't do weekend camps anymore. These were great crack and brought so many together for total fun,' he concludes.

The ChildVision campus has been home to camps and student exchanges for more years than I care to remember. I recall the late 60s fun as the pupils from St Vincent's School for the Blind in Liverpool camped out in our cow field.

As part of a Braille reading expedition, I spent a fantastic weekend at Vincent's in May 1970. We couldn't stop playing soccer, snooker and debating the social issues of the day.

In recent years I have been a guest at the ChildVision July summer camps organised by Raymond McSweeney, Anne Marie Costello and Alex Whelan. From 2022 to 2027, the ChildVision crew are engaging in an extensive EU Erasmus school transfer programme where sport will take prime place.

I also supported the Camp Abilities Easter weeks at Cappalea in Kerry, organised by Active Disabilities Ireland. Niamh Daffy, then CEO, imported the American-style camp in 2010.

In recent years, Camp Abilities has moved north to Limerick and is run by Vision Ireland's Children's Unit with active support from Vision Sports Ireland. The current menu of activities includes rock-climbing, canoeing, kayaking, orienteering, soccer, goalball, judo, swimming, horse riding and tennis.

Annie Donnelly (15) from Horse and Jockey in Tipperary is a Camp Abilities veteran. She says, 'It's fun and inclusive. I have attended four camps, and each year is different. Last year, they introduced horse riding. In the evenings, we had a spa night, and we had our nails painted. I like that it is different every year. I'm done now with camp activities participation, but I hope to go back in future years as a leader.'

At the closing of Capabilities in April 2023, Annie recited her self-penned ditty entitled 'Our Camp Abilities':

We were given a challenge,
We were given disabilities.
They gave us a solution,
They gave us Camp Abilities.

Unpack your bag,
Chat to your campmate.
Try to get some sleep,
Breakfast at half eight.

From county to county,
And hellos over screens.
We were made feel safe,
By any means.

We tried the new,
We tried the old.
We sweat in the heat,
We froze in the cold.

Venture in water,
Venture in land.
Struggle at all,
Help is at hand.

Thank you for the fun,
Thanks to the people here.
Leaving now,
I shed a tear.'

4. Heroes

Two centuries ago.

Three visionaries from yesteryear laid the foundations for modern organised sport for b/vi people. Collectively, these three nineteenth-century boys were world-renowned for b/vi welfare, education, employment, advocacy and philanthropy. We know them for their sporting lives and developing physical education for b/vi people.

Thomas Rhodes Armitage (1824–1890), who began losing his sight in his late thirties, possibly due to childhood typhoid, was an accomplished swimmer and member of the Tipperary Hunt. He championed the universal acceptance of Braille as a reading and writing format for b/vi people. He founded what is now the Royal National Institute for the Blind (RNIB). His daughter, Alice, founded the National Council for the Blind of Ireland (now Vision Ireland), which is home to our national governing body, Vision Sports Ireland.

Sir Francis Joseph Campbell (1832–1914) from Tennessee, who lost his sight when he walked into an acacia tree as a toddler, was the first b/vi person to climb Mont Blanc. He was also a talented musician who turned his talents to become a world-leading educator.

Samuel Gridley Howe (1801–1875) was a military revolutionary and surgeon who founded the world-famous Perkins School for the Blind in his hometown, Boston. Of note, his philanthropic support came from Colonel Thomas Handasyd Perkins, a slave trader and opium smuggler. Howe was the first great coach of b/vi sports and leisure.

Were Armitage, Campbell, and Howe to be reincarnated today, chances are they would be leading the world in developing sport for disabled people, from beginner/light leisure activities to high-performance para-sports.

On opening the Perkins School in 1832, Samuel Gridley Howe viewed the students' poor health as a serious source of concern. Two centuries ago, most children who were b/vi in the western world were treated as invalids and prevented from doing anything for themselves. Fearing injury, their families and local communities discouraged them from enjoying physical activity. In India and other parts of the world, b/vi people were often ostracised and told to atone for their sins.

At Perkins, Howe knew how: Get 'em up at 6.30 am each day and put 'em under pressure through short bursts of physical and intellectual activity. The drill recovery intervals facilitated time to mingle, eat and drink.

The results were immediate and positive. Howe went further and introduced miles and miles of walking, running and sea-swimming two centuries ahead of his time!

Meanwhile, the 'playground movement' was the way to go for Sir Francis Campbell, a Perkins teacher on a European sabbatical. His goal: 'To discover and arrange suitable games and outdoor sports, which would offer irresistible attractions for the blind,' making physical fitness enjoyable.

Following a chance meeting with Thomas Armitage in London, the main man and conduit for all that moved in western world b/vi affairs, Campbell's plan ignited. Together, they founded the Royal Normal College in London – now the Royal National College (RNC) – where Campbell was installed as director. With Armitage's financial backing, they built an accessible gym – the envy of the British empire – as well as skating rinks, a swimming pool and a playground bigger than Windsor Castle and its grounds.

Over at Worcester College, a boarding school for blind and sighted sons of gentlemen and Church of England clergymen, they were not keen on exercise drills. Instead, they played with a large improvised wickerwork sound football called 'the Moon'. They also played single-wicket cricket and a game called 'Blood and Thunder', which required hockey sticks. In calmer moments, they rowed and swam in the nearby river. They also practised athletics and gymnastics and enjoyed long country walks. The popular but inexplicably short-lived annual sports day included running, jumping, throwing, hammer-throwing and cricket, as well as wheelbarrow and sack races.

All three world-beating colleges – Perkins, RNC and Worcester – are still alive and kicking today. Among notable Perkins past pupils are deaf-blind activists Anne Sullivan and Helen Keller. Former British home secretary David Blunkett is said to have failed his entrance assessment for Worcester but did graduate with honours at RNC (now in Hereford). Our own triple-gold cycling Paralympic star Katie-George Dunlevy attended both colleges.

BBC Sports presenter Gabby Logan, who made her TV debut representing Leeds at the 1991 Rose of Tralee, is a big supporter of the RNC. Gabby, however, would willingly step back to make way for the RNC's most famous supporter, King Charles III.

5. The games people play

A century ago. Early competitions in athletics, cricket, Gaelic games, rowing, skittles and swimming.

While Ireland is now best-in-class in development and innovation of sport for b/vi people, we were worst in class for much of the past two centuries. Harriet Armitage, wife of Thomas Armitage, hailed from Noan, near Cashel, Co. Tipperary. Thomas regularly holidayed here and visited our schools and institutions for b/vi people. However, he couldn't break into Fort Knox!

Our education system, and by extension, extracurricular sport and leisure, was wildly off-pace. It was hamstrung by finance, religion, social attitudes and politics. It operated without any reference to significant developments in Europe and the USA. In fact, of the six Irish schools/institutions for b/vi people that emerged during the nineteenth century, just two exist to this day.

St Joseph's in Drumcondra, Dublin, was founded in 1858. On its campus, you can now find St Joseph's Primary School for Children with Visual Impairment and Rosmini Community School (for post-primary b/vi and mainstream students). You'll also find ChildVision, which provides facilities for b/vi children and young adults, some of whom also have profound sensory impairments and additional disabilities. The second surviving school is the Ulster Society, founded in Belfast but now in Jordanstown, Co. Antrim, which was established in 1831.

A century ago, schools and homes for b/vi people were known as asylums, places of refuge. By the time I got to St Joseph's as a pupil in the 1960s, it was no longer officially known as an asylum. However, at nearby Tolka Park, home to Premier League of Ireland soccer club Shelbourne, I recall irate fans advising many referees to go back to the blind asylum!

While Ireland was in the education and recreation backwoods, the rest of the world didn't wait. The early twentieth century saw health and fitness skyrocket for b/vi children and youth as team sports and athletic competitions came into play.

On 16 May 1908 thirteen schools participated in the 'first outdoor contest of the National Athletic Association of the Schools for the Blind in the USA'. The events included shot-put, standing broad jump, standing high jump, three standing jumps, running broad jump, 50-yard dash, football throw, 50-yard three-legged race, and 50-yard sack race.

From inter-blind school competitions to taking on mainstream high schools, Perkins in Boston was a pioneer yet again. On 12 March 1912 its boys hammered a team from Framingham High School in an indoor track meet. So thrilled were the Perkins boys that they took on all-comers from high schools across the north-east of the United States and usually won.

To help, fair play adaptations were allowed. Just as today, totally blind players, with guides, can challenge able-bodied competitors in athletics and without guides in swimming. In ball games, the totally blind competitor could be accompanied. Sighted opponents could not tackle without a prior verbal call. B/vi players were also favoured by their teams for spot kicks. If you can't join them, beat them. So it was that the east-coast b/vi girls laid down their cheerleading flags and took to competitive running, swimming and dance. Ahead of the boys, ahead of their time.

Across the pond, in England in 1923, Manchester united to form the first club for b/vi adults. If you had 10 shillings (now worth €20) you could be a member of a club 'of the blind, for the blind, run by the blind'. Indoors, Braille card games were popular, as well as the raised square board game of draughts. They also played dominos, bagatelle and ring-throwing. Outdoors, they engaged with Manchester Corporation, which provided them with an area at the local Heaton Park, complete with a pavilion, skittle alley and cricket pitch. This ground was shut off from the rest of the park, and sighted people could only enter with special permission!

The Manchester and District Social Club entertained b/vi groupings with sports days followed by social evenings. During Easter 1929 they hosted fourteen men and seven women from the Royal Glasgow Blind Asylum in a weekend of contests in a variety of sports, including cricket and skittles, followed by evening social events such as whist drives and dances. The Scots won all by a cricket score, except cricket.

On 14 June 1935 the newly formed British Federation of Social Clubs for the Blind organised the first international athletics meet in Edinburgh, where Scotland beat England.

At junior level, Worcester College students were beating UK all-comers in rowing, athletics and swimming. They had a sub-11-second, 100-yard sprinter and a young discus competitor who could throw to 36 metres. After receiving special permission from the London Athletics Club Committee, their sprinter competed in the open International Public Schools Sports at White City, where he finished a highly credible tenth out of forty-eight competitors.

An interesting film that did the rounds pre-World War Two was called *Grit*. It starred Captain Gerald Lowry, who had no sight, engaging in various sports, including boxing, swimming, exercising with a punchball, running, dancing and playing bridge.

Closer to home, the National League of the Blind of Ireland, aka 'the League', was rocking. With an orchestra, *céilí* bands and many talented musicians, dancing was in full swing. To prove the League was a theatre of dreams, they hosted a football match between Manchester United and Bohemians at Dublin's Dalymount Park to mark their golden jubilee in 1948.

They also held outings and sports days from Dublin to surrounding counties, sometimes travelling by tandem cycle.

The late Paddy McNicholas, a leading b/vi campaigner of the time, told me how the League bought their own tandems during this period. Forty years later, on realising these had rusted and found tandem heaven, Paddy arranged sponsorship to cover the purchase of three brand-new ones for a new generation of b/vi cyclists.

By the mid-twentieth century, the wheels were turning in Ireland.

6. This used to be my playground

School for blind boys with Des Kenny (Kildare) and Philip Doyle (Mayo) including basketball, board games, crab football, cricket, paper ball, swimming and trolley racing.

For almost a century, beginning in the mid-1800s, the catholic Carmelite Brothers took care of St Joseph's as an adult home and later school for b/vi children.

Other than card games, reading, running and the beginnings of board games, such as chess and draughts, little is known about pre-1930s 'Joeys'' recreational activities. In the 30s and 40s, the name of the game was Gaelic football. My dad spoke of inter-provincial Gaelic football among the boys from the four provinces as well as regular kickabouts with the boys from the local north Dublin community.

Legendary GAA and racing commentator Michael O'Hehir lived nearby and took part in many of these games. Later, he would give special mention to the boys of St Joseph's in his famous All-Ireland radio and TV commentaries. Another local family, the Copelands, joined in the games. It is not known if Louis Copeland, the legendary tailor, kitted the boys out in suits and top hats for the big games!

In 1955 the Carmelites ceded power to the Rosminian Order. The Rosminians focused exclusively on the school and arranged for adults to be rehomed, many to the neighbouring Clonturk

House. They engaged in active fundraising, sold some of the unused land for commercial housing and used the proceeds to develop school facilities.

Between 1961 and 1965 the Rosminians built a new school and indoor and outdoor recreation areas. With significant funding from the Variety Club of Ireland, they opened a swimming pool and gym. In 1970 a new 175-metre tarmacadam running track with an infield basketball court was built with proceeds from a private bequest.

While almost all children learned to swim in St Joseph's, there was no formal coaching. Twice a week, the under-10s and under-14s competed in swimming-ladder competitions. From an initial seeding position, those on the even numbers challenged those above them on the uneven numbers on day one; on day two, those on the uneven numbers challenged those above them. Each swim discipline had its own ladder. The June swim gala was the annual pool highlight.

Five-times chess Olympian and a past pupil at St Joseph's (1963–8) Philip Doyle recalls RTÉ and Olympian Brendan O'Reilly filming at the new swimming pool in the mid-60s: 'Where I'm from in the west of Ireland, few had TVs. However, a neighbour of mine told of seeing us on her black-and-white TV, while a Dublin friend said we looked as if we were all swimming in the nude!' (No, the TV programme wasn't called *Naked Camera!*) St Joseph's had a 40 x 2-metre wooden veranda, walled on one side and railed on the other. We called it 'the Shade'. Here, the game of blind man's buff was popular. The Shade also hosted 'paper ball' contests using DIY tennis-size balls made of tough brown paper held together with Sellotape or twine. This was an end-to-end game where players punched the ball, scoring when an opponent failed to save. It worked for totally blind players who felt special awareness, and a level of silence was optimal.

Another end-to-end game is recalled by Des Kenny, a pupil at St Joseph's between 1957 and 1964 and later CEO of NCBI (1986–14). Des comments: 'It was called "basket ball", but not as you know it. The ball was made of basketwork, covered with cloth, with bells inside. You rolled or threw the ball along the grass, aiming to beat the opposing goalie. A belt of the heavy ball could wreck your shins. Splinters from the basketry were common.

'Trolley racing was another dangerous activity we enjoyed. It was a board on ball-bearing wheels and an optional butter box in front to protect your feet. The seat was part of a kitchen chair with the legs removed and the back of the chair left for comfort. The boys used the back of the chair to push you.

'Activities like basketball and trolley racing toughened you up. Fear would never prevent you from participation.'

In the modern era, these sports would be banned – what a pity!

Less dangerous was the team contact 'crab football', which was the number-one indoor sport when I was at St Joseph's (1964–74). The leagues and knockout competitions were fiercely fought. Players supported themselves on their hands and moved with their feet in motions that made them look like crabs. Both totally blind and partially-sighted players had equal status, with all following the echoing sound of the large plastic ball.

Des Kenny, who has no sight following a childhood accident, explains, 'You worked your way into the many scrums; it was survival of the fittest after that!'

Cricket, croquet and conquers were also very popular.

'We played cricket with a rubber ball,' recalls Philip Doyle. 'Totally blind and partially-sighted boys could compete. Paddy Mason, a totally blind lad from Limerick, knew all the tricks. He would kneel with his shot bat angled in front to protect the wicket. It was near impossible to take him out, but, somehow, players did.'

St Joseph's had a vast compendium of adapted board games: chess, draughts, snakes and ladders, bagatelle and card games. Games of rings, skittles and marbles were also popular.

Philip Doyle was a pinball wizard. He recalls: 'Paddy Mullen was our handyman, and he was great at improvising. He assembled a bagatelle board for us. The skillset was to measure how to get the marbles to the best positions.'

Philip recalls the Airfix Betta Bilda range from the 1960s and 70s. 'The boys would build entire mini villages from foundations to roofs and a spire for the mandatory church. We used to take the bricks and build football pitches and flick ludo buttons end to end!'

Aside from Betta Bilda villages, which were sometimes supplemented by Lego, the boys of St Joseph's built an entire Airfix warship. They also built two Hornby electric model train sets, each of which occupied up to 40 sq. metres in recreation areas for many years.

'It was all highly educational,' says Philip. 'How else could a blind person know what a train, ship or boat looked like? It fascinated us.'

There were no football pitches in St Joseph's until the mid-70s. Instead, football matches were played in a field where cows grazed – players landing in shit was quite common! One afternoon when the ref blew the whistle early to accommodate the cows, the shit hit the fan. An irate pupil, Billy Shanahan from Thurles, Tipperary, marched up to the bursar's office, enquiring whether he was in St Joseph's School for Blind Boys or blind cows.

In a case of breaking moos, Billy won the day, and the cows entered pastures new.

7. In a lifetime

Athletes Jim Gallagher (Mayo) and Michael Delaney (Dublin), including tandem cycling, marathons and track and field.

It was 'Hello, goodbye' when I entered St Joseph's in Drumcondra in the mid-60s as Jimmy Gallagher was about to jump the exit gate. At that point, his partial sight was fast fading into total blindness.

I recall a fascinating childhood chat with Jimmy as he spoke of farming life in his native Keenagh, Co. Mayo, particularly his love of horses. Jimmy is a legend of Irish b/vi sport. He could turn his head, hands and feet to anything from ultra-running to ultra-organisation.

Sadly, Jimmy passed away on his seventy-fifth birthday on 12 November 2020. I was honoured that my written tribute was read out at his funeral mass. The final words read, 'Jimmy Gallagher – we guess you never knew how you did it, but you did it. Thank you, and rest in peace.'

Jimmy Gallagher was Ireland's first blind marathon runner. He completed thirty-six including the first Dublin City Marathon, with a best time of three hours and fifteen minutes. Jimmy set the pace, and hundreds of us b/vis took to the Dublin City Marathon thereafter. Six years ago I approached organisers Jim Aughney and Eugene Coppinger and asked them to create an official category for b/vi runners. They did so immediately and also provided very generous prize money.

A decade ago Jimmy Gallagher told me of his 1996 Chicago Marathon run, where CNN conducted a *live* interview with him. While he had a CD copy of the 45-second insert, it could not play due to its old format. Jimmy was so appreciative when I converted the footage to a generic format. The interview can be viewed on the Vision Sports Ireland YouTube channel.

On leaving St Joseph's, Jim took to the gym. In late 1960s Ireland, gyms were basic with loose weights left lying around. Regulars watched in awe as Jimmy weaved his way around the obstacle course. He was among the strongest and fittest of them all.

In between long-distance runs, Jimmy loved his regular European skiing holidays with English and Northern Irish-based groupings. He also skied across Italy with Vision Ireland. He was a regular on local tandem and walking tours with Louth WATCH (Walking and Tandem Cycling Club for Health). He cycled the world with Vision Ireland's infamous and now-defunct Blazing Saddles fundraising group. Shortly before his death, Jimmy could be found boxing with Vision Ireland's Iona Centre in Dublin.

Jimmy was ever-present in the development of nationally organised sport for b/vi people in Ireland. He played a crucial role in attracting BBC/RTÉ broadcaster Liam Nolan to chair the founding meeting of Vision Sports Ireland in November 1988.

In May 2014 Jimmy Gallagher became the first athlete to be inducted into the Vision Sports Ireland Hall of Fame. Whenever, wherever you meet b/vi sportspeople, Jimmy Gallagher's name pops up as a key life influencer.

Another name which glides off many lips is Michael Delaney. From sprints to marathons, from para-triathlons to chess championships, Michael Delaney simply oozed talent.

In 1993 he won European bronze in the high jump at the International Blind Sports Federation (IBSA) European Athletics Championships in Dublin. He represented Ireland at three Paralympic Games (1996, 2000 and 2008) and two Braille Chess Paralympiads (1992 and 2004). He was a tandem cycling pioneer and competed in Beijing 2008. Five years later, he was Ireland's first international para-triathlete when he competed in the world championships in London.

My favourite Michael Delaney story is about the day he returned to the dressing room after a short sprint session. He got into a slagging match with Raheny Shamrocks club mates who had just completed a long run in preparation for a marathon. 'Easy for you, Mick,' they teased. 'You're out there for an hour. We've just run twenty miles in almost three hours!' Mick asked them when their marathon was. 'Eight weeks' time,' came the reply. 'No bother,' *sez* Mick. 'See *ya* there.' From sprints to a marathon in two months, Mick did it in style, clocking just over three hours.

Michael Delaney fought a tough illness and left us far too early in May 2020. A year later, he was posthumously inducted into the Vision Sports Ireland Hall of Fame. There's no doubt there's one hell of an Irish b/vi sports team in heaven with Jimmy Gallagher and Michael Delaney calling the shots.

8. School's out

School for blind girls with Sr Brid (Clare), Carol Carr (Dublin), Catherine Walsh (Dublin) and Katie-George Dunlevy (Donegal/UK) including athletics, rounders and swimming.

For 143 years the Sisters of Charity ran St Mary's School for Visually Impaired Girls in Merrion, in south-east Dublin. School's out now since 2001, as the sisters passed the baton on to the education centre north of the Liffey on the ChildVision campus in Drumcondra. St Mary's school and home was surrounded by 33 acres of picturesque prime estate, including a river and lake, just a fifteen-minute walk from the beaches of the Irish Sea.

In 1982, at the invite of pioneering school principal Sr Kevin, now Sr Brid, I visited Merrion to discuss the global revolution in sport for b/vi people. Forty years later, in July 2022, I re-visited Sr Brid, now ninety-four. Just like in 1982, she was helpful and oh so proud of her past pupils, including the Paralympians. For the record, two of her pupils won Paralympic gold medals while none of the rival St Joseph's boys have ever won gold!

Sr Brid recalled the reaction to the idea of building a swimming pool at Merrion six decades ago when people mused, 'Swimming pool for blind children, do you want to drown them?'

She added, 'All things come to those who wait, so the right time did come. Without the help of the knowledgeable men of the Variety Club of Ireland, the pool would never have materialised.'

Sr Brid credits Chief Barker Rick Burke, top dog at Variety through the 1960s and 70s, for providing £35,000 (€750,000 today) to part-fund the pool. Variety also funded gym and playground facilities. 'Rick took a shine to me. We were great friends. Anything I asked for, he delivered.' Variety also supported St Joseph's with their pool and sports equipment.

In February 1966 Dr Patrick Hillary, a future president of Ireland, opened the Merrion pool. It was no surprise to see Dr Hillary at the opening, as his dad had delivered Sr Brid into this world. Sr Brid and Dr Hillary were childhood neighbours in Milltown Malbay, Co. Clare.

PE, gymnastics and dancing were popular at Sr Brid's state-of-the-art Merrion gym. Out in the field, athletics, tandem cycling and basketball, with occasional mountain climbing and sports days, also trended.

Ireland's first b/vi Paralympic gold medallist Carol Carr remembers her introduction to sport at Merrion: 'I absolutely loved rounders, which is like mini cricket, where a standard bat and football was used. As I'm partially-sighted, I joined in helping girls with no vision to bat, run and fully participate.'

Catherine Walsh, who has competed in a record seven Paralympic Games, was a pupil at Merrion from age ten. 'We had lots of activities there but nothing competitive. We never entered inter-schools' competitions. Merrion was close to the UCD running track, where Irish Blind Sports held Saturday sports training. We loved going there to meet the boys. We had a teacher, a runner, Caitriona NicGiollaeoin, who supported us as we did our midweek training on Sandymount beach and around the Merrion's extensive grounds.'

Merrion, the school, is gone, but Sr Brid still lives on its grounds in retirement. Among her prized possessions is a recording and photograph of her pupils singing their way to the top of the pop charts with 1960s superstar Butch Moore as they belted out 'Santa Claus is Coming to Town'.

Few children nowadays attend blind schools in western Europe as integrated mainstream education is now the way to go. But past pupils speak highly of such schools, particularly when it came to sport.

Triple Irish Paralympic gold star and tandem stoker Katie-George Dunlevy attended mainstream school up to age thirteen in 1995.

'I was struggling at mainstream. In the sports hall, I thought I could see, but I was running into people and missing the ball. Later, after my RP [retinitis pigmentosa] diagnosis, I remember being left out of PE class, which was my favourite lesson. I was left sitting on the side, although the teachers did try to help me.

'Once my eyesight problem was diagnosed, it gave me a reason for my struggles. I knew I wasn't stupid. I was as good as anyone else. It was just, I couldn't see as good as them. It was hard to accept, though, and I didn't like being put at the top of the class to see the blackboard. I remember driving my parents mad by sitting in the back seat of the car going to school and constantly chanting, "I can see, I can see, I can see."'

It all changed for UK-based Katie once her parents, John and Alana, enrolled her at Dorton House school for b/vi children in Kent, an hour's drive from her home in Crawley.

'I was a day pupil for the first year but then boarded, as I loved the school. They encouraged me to do loads of different sports. I did a PE GCSE.

'The facilities at Dorton House were fantastic. We had a 400-metre running track, all-weather pitches and a large swimming pool. Out of school hours, I also did windsurfing and rowing, and I even tried the tandem bike. We also went away skiing.'

From her Dorton House base, Katie soon began competing nationally and internationally.

With her tandem cycling partner Eve McCrystal, they won the 2021 RTÉ Sports Team of the Year, beating off competition from the Ireland rugby and All-Ireland winning teams. Two years later, Katie, this time with pilot Linda Kelly, was again nominated for the prestigious award.

Looking back at her school days, Katie says, 'I didn't want to go to boarding school, but I settled in because I got into the sport. Everything fell into place; they had great facilities. I went from having low self-esteem to being more confident.'

Without a doubt, boarding schools for b/vi people have left an impressive sports legacy.

9. Top of the world

Para-cyclist Katie-George Dunlevy (Donegal/UK), including downhill skiing, para-rowing, swimming and tandem cycling.

Beat this:
- Ireland's most successful para-cyclist ever
- Ireland's most successful female Paralympian of the twenty-first century
- Ireland's most successful female b/vi Paralympian ever
- Winner, with cycling partners Eve McCrystal and Linda Kelly, of twelve gold, nine silver and three bronze medals at Paralympic Games, UCI World Para-cycling and European Championships

And the beat goes on as super champ Katie-George Dunlevy heads for Paris 2024 with the goal of more gold.

Katie had sight loss as a child and was diagnosed with retinitis pigmentosa (RP) at age eleven. She was told she could have no sight by age thirty. Thankfully, she still has a small degree of useful vision and had cataracts removed a decade ago.

Katie's first taste of competition was poolside three decades ago while boarding at Dorton House, the school for b/vi children in Kent (see #8). One day, her PE teacher Graham Ruck asked her mum, 'Who taught Katie to swim?'

'Nobody,' replied her mum. 'She taught herself by watching her older sisters.'

'She's a natural,' Graham Ruck responded. 'I'd love her to get coaching and enter her into competitions.'

To this day, Katie says Graham was her greatest influence.

Graham's coaching and Katie's skills soon yielded results as she became an all-round national swim champion in events for b/vi youth. Katie competed in Europe and represented the UK at underage long-course championships in Barcelona. She then moved on to excel at downhill skiing. Once familiar with the slopes, Katie was on her own with a guide. She recalls:

'Between Dorton House and, later, Worcester College in the UK, I went on five ski trips, including two trips to the Rockies in Colorado with the World Skiing Club for the Disabled. It was through British Blind Sports that I was able to compete in many sports, including athletics, swimming and skiing.'

Illness interrupted Katie's academic and sporting career, but a new sporting opportunity soon arose.

'I got a call from the GB para-rowing coach inviting me to trial for their national squad for this new sport. They planned to compete in the 2004 World Championships with the goal of participating in Beijing 2008.

'I jump at any opportunity, so I took up the challenge. While quite unfit, I passed the rowing-machine tests and joined the squad. Each weekend I travelled from my university base in Southampton to East London to train. The rowing was very tough, technical, and so competitive!

'The GB team competed in the world championships in Spain, and we won gold! A year later, in Japan, we won again! These two world golds were achieved with the GB mixed coxed four team, all b/vi rowers. In 2006 the rules changed, and the coxed four teams included physical disability rowers. I was selected for the boat in the 2006 World Championships in Dorney. I tried out but failed to be selected in 2009 and 2010.'

Since childhood, Katie has been a frequent visitor to Ireland as her dad, John, is from Mountcharles in Donegal. She competed in athletics at Mayfest in Dublin in the late 1990s and recalls having her photo taken with Irish Paralympic star Catherine Walsh. Her Irish links and connections were soon to yield an unexpected bonus.

'In 2010 I joined the Irish para-rowing squad. A year later, I missed out on qualifying for London 2012. By now, I was emotionally and mentally done and just wanted to go home. I was continuously, narrowly missing out on the dream of the Paralympics.

'Out of the blue the para-rowing manager, Joe Cunningham, said the para-cycling team was watching me and was very interested. Joe introduced me to Brian Nugent at Cycling Ireland.

'I had no background in cycling, but they saw something in me. I had no gear and no helmet, and used a large men's tandem, which I kept falling off of.

'Six weeks later I was racing at the UCI World Para-cycling Championships in Denmark. I loved it, the adrenaline, speed, just so exciting.

'London 2012 was my pinch-me moment. I just couldn't believe I had made it and on a tandem. Cycling at Brands Hatch with my pilot Sandra FitzGerald, with thousands of spectators cheering us on, was simply amazing. I was disappointed we didn't win a medal, but we were close.'

A year later Katie teamed up with Eve McCrystal. They punctured in the time trial and a few days later won their first medal at the UCI World Championships in Greenville, USA, in

2014. 'A photo finish, it was silver, but it felt like gold. The screams from me made everyone think we had won,' says Katie.

2015 was marred by injury and illness, so going into Rio 2016, Katie and Eve were seeded fifth for the women's time trial. 'We had a fantastic ride but were exhausted and laid on the floor at the finish. We knew we had given it everything. Then the wait, as the higher-seeded bikes raced, but none could beat our time. Gold! Absolute elation. My twelve years of trials and tribulations flashed before me in an instant.'

Rio also had a silver-medal lining in the road race.

Now Paralympic road champions Katie and Eve set sights on world titles. From 2017 to 2022 they won gold six times. In 2021 they lost out on gold, not once, but twice, at the UCI World Para-Cycling Road Championships in Portugal. Katie says, 'Sometimes losing is a good thing. It makes you step up. When you lose, you analyse better. Three months later, we turned up fully prepared at the Tokyo Paralympics and won gold in both the time trial and road race. Defending the Paralympic time trial title was pressurised. We were confident, we liked the course, and we were willing to hurt to win. We won by a huge margin.

'The second gold on the road was tighter. The wet conditions left Eve slightly nervous with tough, sloping roads and tight bends on a course we didn't know. Towards the end, there were three tandems in the leading group. It became highly tactical as we knew the others were fast finishers, and we needed to find a way to get away. On the last of ten laps, Eve identified the gap, we went for it and led to the line. Gold!'

Katie and Eve added a silver on the track – astonishing, considering they had very little track time, as Ireland still awaits its first velodrome.

Sport has been good to Katie, and she's been good for sport, especially inclusion in sport. 'It gives me huge purpose in life, but it's not me either and doesn't totally make me. It has given me so much fulfilment and confidence, especially in my earlier years. It will always be a big part of my life.'

Katie has a long and winding road to Paris '24 and is planning for that pot of gold once more.

10. To see or not to see

Vision-impaired classes with Paralympics Ireland classification manager Ana Maia (Brazil/Ireland).

While promoting the 2019 Maynooth Students for Charity Galway Cycle for Vision Sports Ireland, I was interviewed on KFM (Kildare local radio) and explained I had 10 per cent vision. As we returned home, my co-interviewee, former Vision Sports director Bernie Everard, said in surprise: 'Nobody in Maynooth [our hometown] will believe you have just 10 per cent sight; they'll be shocked.'

Many b/vi people find their low levels of sight, even no sight, can be misunderstood; mostly overestimated but sometimes underestimated too. (I visit the phenomenon of misunderstood and invisible disability in detail with Paralympic star Jason Smyth later. For now, let's check out how the scientists and sports classifiers see us.)

To compete in para-sports – sports which may be adapted from able-bodied or have been specifically created for athletes with a vision impairment – athletes must first undergo an evaluation called classification. The assessment for athletes with a vision impairment considers the visual acuity of the better eye while wearing best optical correction using either spectacles or contact lenses and/or visual fields, which include central and peripheral zones.

To determine visual acuity, your journey might begin with the ophthalmologist's eye chart, the log of the minimum angle of resolution (LogMAR), a chart with fourteen lines of sets of five words beginning in large font and ever-decreasing to the bottom line. Each letter has a value, with the highest scores for the large ones. If you miss the large ones using your better eye with correction (spectacles/contact lenses), you score high. For classification, a chart with the letter E in different sizes and directions is used to determine the LogMAR. High scores mean a greater level of impairment and potential eligibility for para-sport; the lower the score, the closer the athlete is to the mainstream.

To find your visual range, your ophthalmologist may request a visual field test relevant to your impairment. This test assesses how wide of an area you can see when you focus on a central point with either eye. The eye specialist may ask you to look directly at an object in front of you, such as their eye/nose/hands, while one of your eyes is covered. They may hold up different numbers of fingers in areas of your side vision field and ask how many you see as you look at the target in front of you. This test might also be carried out using a visual field machine.

Ana Maia has vast experience in para-sport, with an encyclopaedic knowledge of all disability classifications. She attended her first Paralympic Games at London 2012 with the Brazil team. Subsequently, she moved home to Ireland and worked with the Ireland team in Rio 2016 and Tokyo 2020. As the classification manager at Paralympics Ireland, she is best placed to explain the process. 'Success in competition is determined by skill and ability, not impairment. Vision-impairment classifications are there to ensure a level playing field where athletes are divided into categories called classes according to the level of impairment they have. Athletes with similar levels of activity limitation compete against each other within each class, and therefore, totally blind athletes don't compete against athletes with partial or 20/20 vision.'

Armed with your ophthalmologist's report, you may fit into one of the three universally accepted sports competition categories of B1, B2 or B3, where 'B' identifies blindness:

B1: Visual acuity lower than LogMAR 2.6; B2: visual acuity ranging from LogMAR 1.5 to 2.6 (inclusive) and/or visual field constricted to a diameter of less than 10 degrees; B3: visual acuity ranging from LogMAR 1.4 to 1.0 (inclusive) and/or visual field constricted to a diameter of less than 40 degrees.

An example of a B1 competitor would be Ireland's first blind marathon man, Jimmy Gallagher. Jimmy had no sight and always required a guide while running. Our first Paralympic gold medallist, Carol Carr, was a B2 competitor. She could have availed of a guide but was comfortable without. However, she has a guide dog for day-to-day navigation. Jason Smyth – who can see the track but cannot identify detail – is in category B3.

As if it isn't complicated enough, some bright spark came up with B4 and B5 categories for those who narrowly miss the bus but still wish to stay on track. B4 excludes visual field range and is based on a LogMAR acuity reading of better than 1.0 up to and including 0.6. B5 facilitates sight greater than B4. Thereafter, interpretations may vary. B4 and B5 classes are not officially recognised in competitive para-sport.

Thankfully, we leave it to the classifiers to determine our category. At senior competitions, such as the Paralympic Games, you must pass the Irish national classifier and the international classifier, as well as attending pre-competition validations. It's a fair, well-honed process, which leaves room for reviews and appeals.

Away from high-performance sport, it's more flexible. Vision Sports Ireland and British Blind Sports, our sport's governing bodies on this island, welcome all with sight impairment. However, they would like you to register with the relevant registration bodies, such as Vision Ireland or RNIB.

So, now you know: you can't rock up, tell the eyesight classifier you can't see the chart, never mind its letters, and take the next plane to the Paralympic Games.

While gathering the stories for this book, I asked every b/vi contributor for details on their eye condition and level of sight. All were very happy to do so. However, I was reminded of RTÉ radio's *Listen and See* Sunday evening programme, where host Jim Sherwin always asked b/vi interviewees how much they could see. Our first sports secretary, Eamonn Madden, who had albinism with partial sight, gave Jim the classic answer,

'I can see 93 million miles, Jim; I can see the sun!'

11. Jump!

My early days.

My first two long jumps were the hop, skip and fall. My final effort landed me on a garden rake. I was down and out with a few scratches.

Early bath then …

'Come back,' said Fr Murphy in his harsh Scottish accent. 'It's my fault, sorry, you can go again at the end of the competition.'

It was my first school sports day at St Joseph's in Drumcondra in June 1965. I was a plump eight-year-old city kid, while John Joe Reynolds was a tall, muscular and experienced athlete.

John Joe slid through the muddy sand pit and long jumped 6 feet 8 inches. The gold medal was his.

Then, Fr Murphy remembered I had an extra jump. I have relived that jump a million times. 6 feet 10 inches! The winner!

A two-metre hop, that's all it was. A few years later, Bob Beaman jumped 8.95 metres at the 1968 Mexico Olympics. Bob's massive jump is now seen as a small step for mankind, but my little leap was a giant step into sport for me.

As for Fr Murphy, it may have been the long jump in 1965, but twenty-three years later he ensured I completed the high jump as he officiated at my marriage to Grainne.

I was born at St Kevin's Hospital, now St James's, in Dublin, on 6 September 1956. For my first thirty years, my home was in the nearby working-class suburb of Drimnagh.

While my mum, Julia, and my older sister, Julie, had normal sight, my dad, Paddy, and my older brother, Chris, had congenital cataracts.

Like my dad and my brother, I was born totally blind. From the ages of three to seven I had seven relatively successful operations to break up those cataract sight blockers. The result was enough sight, maybe 10 per cent, to let me see as if I was looking through a steamed-up window.

My mum and dad weren't into sport. Maybe it was the gardaí back in the 1930s who put my dad off by trying to return him to the asylum, or a broken leg later, but he couldn't kick ball for nuts. Instead, he was a deft woodworker and basket-maker with a keen interest in organising accordion bands and music in general.

My mum was the go-to person in our area for knitting, crocheting, darning, sewing and whatever you're having yourself.

In Drimnagh, in the summer of 1965, I was jumping from sport to sport in what we called 'the Dump', our field of dreams, now called Brickfield Park. Like many of my generation, when Wimbledon came on telly we were out the door with saws and hatches making wooden tennis rackets. Then cricket; those bats were much easier to make. And then the showjumping. Wow! That had it all as we took to the jumps.

We built our own obstacle courses using kitchen chairs and brush handles, as well as the U-shaped grass container for the water jump. You just could not afford to clip this jump as you'd be hit by a double whammy: A drowning and a nasty bruise after the whack on the back of your leg.

Our biggest water jump was diving into the nearby Grand Canal for a post-soccer match swim.

While I was midfield maestro and captain at boarding school, it was different in the Dump, where I felt I wasn't up to it. Years later, my friends told me I was always near the top of the selection list because I ran like a hare while others poached around the goal area.

At St Joseph's, where I boarded for nine months each year, sport was all around. In 1969 I was caught on cine-camera overlapping everyone, including much older boys, at the annual sports day walk. I won every annual school sports day walk ever after. Br Summerling, who played a key role in my sports development, said I could be a national walks champion. A step too far for me!

By June 1971 I won everything at that year's sports day. RTÉ star Brendan O'Reilly returned to St Joseph's and presented me with the Champions Cup.

On my fifteenth birthday I jogged the new 175-metre track at St Joseph's. I couldn't stop running until the dinner bell rang. Eighty laps and counting. That was the day I had the feeling that I just might be good at middle-distance running.

Little did I know that later that decade a sports movement would emerge, which would allow me to run against athletes all over the world with similar eyesight to mine.

12. **The letter**

Where national organised sport began, with Martin Kelly (Kildare), featuring athletics.

'Hello, good evening and welcome,' was the standard opening line from the late Jim Sherwin on RTÉ Radio's *Listen and See* on a sunny Sunday evening in July 1978.

'I have a letter from Ann McKay inviting you to attend an athletics competition in Scotland for blind people ...' Our ears pricked as a new frontier opened.

The seeds were sewn, and a dynamic new sports movement soon sprouted in Ireland.

As Jim Sherwin posted his radio invite, Martin Kelly was home alone in Newbridge, Co. Kildare. At the age of seven Martin was diagnosed with macular dystrophy during a routine school medical check-up. While he continued to play sport into adulthood – Gaelic football, hurling, handball and cycling – his sight deterioration led to decreasing exercise levels. He was beginning to feel he was both a couch potato and lounge lizard.

Then, his saviour appeared. He was seduced by the dulcet tones of Ann McKay, who was being interviewed on RTÉ Radio. He wrote her a letter seeking more information. Within months they were an item, and within four years, they married.

Back on track, Martin was one of six Southern Irish lads to set sail for Scotland. He says, 'I knew none of the established b/vi group. It was Gerry Campbell, soon to be one of our sporting legends, who met me at Connolly Station in Dublin and introduced me to my travelling companions.

'It was a fantastic trip to Belfast and Larne by train and then to Stranraer by boat. On then by train along the western Scottish coastline to Glasgow. We met up with participants from across the UK at the Glasgow Central Toby Jug bar.

'Later we boarded the blue-and-yellow Glasgow City Council-sponsored buses for the Queen Margaret Halls. It's a lovely memory, a now historical journey, and while I could never have guessed at the time, that was my first of so many trips there.

'The Scottish Games were held on Saturday 2 September at Grangemouth Stadium in Falkirk, half an hour's drive north of Edinburgh. The events were well organised with competitors from across the UK and Northern Ireland, as well as us,' recalls Martin.

Competitors were separated into two categories: Those who couldn't see and those who could see a little.

Martin recalls being in awe of the totally blind competitors in the 100-metre sprint.

'They had a calling system in place at the time. Their coach or guide had a megaphone and stood at the centre of lane five. The totally blind athlete raced solo from start to finish. The coach or guide would call out "lane 555". The gun blasted, the athlete ran and, if they veered to their left, the call was "lane 444", or right "lane 666" and so on. When the athlete headed towards lanes one or eight, the next call was "stop". This calling system was in place until 1992, and, as far as I know, the call was never "999".'

Martin continued: 'This amazing 100-metre was made even more exciting by a ferocious rivalry between England and Scotland. The main battle was between Graham Salmon [London] and Willie McLeod [Edinburgh]. I remember, after each race, Willie would light up a cigarette at the corner of the track.'

Seven years later, Willie McLeod broke the world record for the 100m at our Dublin May Games at the Morton Stadium in Santry.

Nowadays, the totally blind athlete competing at 100m (and all other track events) is accompanied by a guide. The guide may never step ahead of the blind athlete and must link them using a regulator tether. The way the sport is progressing, Usain Bolt will not be fast enough to guide our best.

B/vi athletes compete in all individual track events, excluding hurdles and steeplechase. Athletes also may not compete in pole vault and hammer. The rules can be found in the International Paralympic Committee (IPC) Handbook, which broadly follows the World Athletics rule book. In general, blind or those with no useful vision avail of qualified guides, while partially sighted athletes may participate without a guide. Athletes now compete in categories T_{11}, F_{11} (B1), T_{12}, F_{12} (B2) and T_{13}, F_{113} (B3) – check out #10 for more on how these categories are established.

So, how did the Irish do at those first Scottish Games? Martin recalls: 'I won the high jump as well as a few running medals. My friend Pat Kelly won the rest of the running events. We did alright!'

Joining Martin, Pat and Gerry on that historic maiden voyage were Tony Scanlon (Tipperary), Tony Sweeney (Limerick) and the late Eamonn Madden (Dublin).

After Scotland '78 Martin joined Newbridge Athletic Club and won medals at middle-distance track at the open Kildare County Championships.

Thanks to organisation and funding by the Irish Wheelchair Association (IWA), Martin represented Ireland at our first

Paralympic Games in Arnhem, the Netherlands, with credible results at 400m, 1500m and javelin.

Twenty years earlier the first Summer Paralympic Games were held in Rome. The seeds for para-sport grew from the sheer volume of World War Two casualties receiving rehabilitation at Stoke Mandeville Hospital in England under the pioneering direction of Dr Ludwig Guttmann.

At the 1972 Paralympic Games in Heidelberg, goalball was a demo sport. Goalball is a team sport for b/vi players, in which a ball containing bells is thrown at goal by opposing teams on an indoor sports hall pitch. Four years later, at the Toronto Paralympics, the sport progressed to competition level.

Two years after Martin Kelly's Paralympic outing – and several international competitions later – he hung up his spikes. He is now in active retirement, exercising on his treadmill, taking long walks and playing vi tennis.

In May 2016 Martin Kelly was inducted into the Vision Sports Ireland Hall of Fame.

13. Hey Frankie

Swim coach Frank Cullinan (Dublin).

'Do you know Dalkey, Joe?' asks Frank Cullinan as we drive into the beautiful South County Dublin seaside village on a hot August morning.

'Sure do, Frank. It's the home of Bono, Binchy and lots of famous people.'

'Bono? He grew up near me in Cedarwood Road in Glasnevin, a brat!' laughs Frank. 'Maeve Binchy? An absolute lady.'

We pull up outside a group of shops, which Frank once owned. 'Maeve bought her flowers from me; she brought flowers for every occasion and function she attended. We lived across the road from each other for several years.'

Frank Cullinan is a retired florist, sales manager and Ireland's number-one disability swim coach. Now aged ninety, with colleague Aoife Drumm, he coaches a dozen or more Vision Sports Ireland members each Friday night at Dublin's Markievicz Pool.

After my guided Dalkey tour, where everyone knew Frank, we adjourned to his beautiful home, where his wife Betty spoiled us with tea and scones.

As a youngster, Frank loved outdoor swimming – no heated pools until the 1950s in Dublin – and cricket, Gaelic football and hurling. He excelled at soccer as a goalkeeper and central defender. (He admits to learning the dark arts of defending at an English seminary but will not admit to using such arts!)

With Postal United, Frank played at all our football stadia and won several trophies through the 1950s and early 60s, including Senior Amateur League Cups.

In 1971 he travelled to England to study and became one of Ireland's first fully certified swim coaches. He coached in competition and high performance. He stepped back from elite swimming in the mid-1970s after witnessing an event that disgusted him.

Frank vividly remembers the pre-teen boy: 'He was a wonderful, highly talented young lad. He was racing and trying as hard as he could with his body going up, down, up, down and back up again, but he was tiring. He was beaten into third place. As he got out of the pool, his angry dad clattered him across the face.'

Frank immediately made the switch from high performance to disability and has never looked back.

At St John of God swimming pool at Kilmainham, Dublin, he trained children and young adults with various disabilities, including intellectual disabilities. He also coached swimmers with levels of blindness. However, he found himself at the deep end when he began coaching at St Mary's School for Blind Girls in Merrion in 1986, at the invite of school principal Sr Claire.

Using his well-honed coaching instructions, he witnessed chaos as the senior girls flip-flopped into the pool, spreading out in all directions. He quickly rescued them and developed an imaginative approach to help the swimmers visualise.

'I used precise audio description to encourage straight-line swimming. I asked them to imagine they were sliding down a rope and following a sidebar. It worked. I had tappers at the end of the pool, so they knew to turn. They were a wonderful group. We had lots of fun and worked hard to get the results.

'Once b/vi swimmers develop awareness of surroundings and learn the basics, practice takes them to where they want to go. It doesn't matter whether it's the backstroke or breaststroke, they can do it all just like anyone else.'

Frank is fully aware of access issues for b/vi swimmers and would like to see pool managers being more proactive in arranging supports, including allocating staff to guide swimmers to and from dressing rooms and at poolside entry points. He feels strategic areas could be better marked using raised and coloured tape.

He believes pool managers could learn much from the Dublin Markiewicz Centre. 'The staff there are simply brilliant. They will do anything for b/vi swimmers. I watch them as they even take care of their guide dogs, wonderful staff.'

While athletics may be the rock on which nationally organised sport for b/vi people began, swimming provides us with the longest-running training activity. The Markievicz sessions started in October 1979 and were organised by the Sports and Social Club at the League. Five decades later, the League leisure swim sessions continue weekly across the Liffey at Belvedere College each Friday lunchtime. Meanwhile, Frank and Aoife run the Vision Sports Ireland swim classes at the Markievicz each Friday night.

Three weeks after our wonderful Dalkey day out, Frank had a fall, lost consciousness and was hospitalised for three months.

Throughout this critical period, Betty was by his side. She cajoled him and played videos from people like us, his friends, as well as people like rugby stars Ronan O'Gara and Tommy Bowe. Frank made a great recovery and returned home to prepare for Christmas.

Sadly, Betty fell suddenly ill and passed away on 18 December 2022. Heaven has a place for Betty, such a warm, engaging lady, Frank's pillar.

Frank is piecing life back together and returned poolside at Markievicz in early 2023. Always up for the challenge, he invited me to be his first pupil on his return. He may be our greatest coach, but there are pupils he can never teach!

Over five decades, Frank has never asked for and never received a cent. He is a coach and volunteer extraordinaire.

In May 2014 Frank Cullinan was inducted into the Vision Sports Ireland Hall of Fame.

14. Here, there, and almost everywhere

Spreading the word with Gerry Campbell (Longford), Anne Kelly, née McKay (Scotland/Kildare) and Des Kenny (Kildare). The early days of national organised sport for b/vi people.

Double Paralympian Gerry Campbell, the curly red-headed live wire from Abbeyshrule, Co. Longford, introduced Martin Kelly to that Scotland-bound team back in 1978.

Gerry, who has 10 per cent sight due to bilateral congenital cataracts, is another past pupil of St Joseph's from the early 1960s to 70s.

He recalls hearing Anne McKay's Scotland invite: 'I was doing a bit of running back then, but nothing organised. I thought going to Scotland could be boring, but I could try. I remember doing the long jump. I hadn't done any specialised training for the long jump, so my take-off and landing were almost to the same spot! I did the shot-put that day, too. I learned so much on the day.

'I got the bug but didn't get to any real level until five years later. In 1983, I represented Ireland at discus at the European Athletics Championships for the Blind in Varna, Bulgaria.'

Gerry subsequently represented his country at the Paralympic Games in New York in 1984 and Seoul in 1988, as well as the IPC World Championships in 1986. He also competed at the European Championships for b/vi athletes in Rome 1985 and Dublin 1993. He holds twelve national titles at discus.

Now retired, Gerry says: 'Getting into sport, training and competing with able-bodied athletes at discus changed my life. I am so grateful to the coaches and athletes who encouraged me. I could go to the Belfield track in Dublin and meet up with some great people. It was fantastic that my colleagues and I could take part in open graded meetings.'

Gerry singles out Scotland Games founder Anne McKay for special mention: 'I can still hear her voice, her lovely accent, on Irish radio back in 1978. My memories are just good memories of her. She was involved in so many things and was such a good organiser. You didn't mess around with Anne. Anyone who tried wouldn't go the second time!'

Anne McKay was born in Dundee, Scotland, with partial eyesight. She played an active role in b/vi advocacy and welfare in Scotland before settling in Ireland in 1980. Anne fought for disability rights in Ireland up to her death on 4 September 2015.

On 21 May 2016 Anne was posthumously inducted into the Vision Sports Ireland Hall of Fame.

Anne's big legacy was firing the starting gun for organised sport for b/vi people in Ireland. With one hop, skip and jump, a giant stride was taken, which saw the founding of our first national sports club. This, in turn, spawned the Sports and Social Club of the 'League', which ultimately gave us Vision Sports Ireland.

In April 1979 Gerry Campbell chaired the first meeting of our Sports Club at the League. There was fire and passion but little money. Thoughts turned to collaborating with the League's social club.

Des Kenny, head of the League from 1974 to 1980, explains: 'I recall supporting various Irish teams travelling to international chess tournaments. It was in my DNA to help such groups, and

I could see the sense of the long-standing League social club merging with the sports side.

'The new competitive-based sports club needed the social side to develop leisure activities like walking and swimming.

'I trusted those involved to know what they were doing, so I helped wherever possible with a hands-off approach. I continued this form of trust and level of support when I joined NCBI. The funded supports were small compared to the overall large budgets for our day-to-day social services work, but it was a vital lifeline for something important to me.'

Soon, the new Sports and Social Club at the League was spreading out in all directions: canoeing at Ballymun pool, swimming at the Markievicz pool in central Dublin, tandem cycling in the Phoenix Park and scuba diving at the ESB Sports Club in Ringsend. At weekends, there were horse-riding classes in Malahide in Dublin and Ashford in Co. Wicklow.

Yes, it was east-coast-centric, largely because most b/vi people were based there. In 1980s Ireland, most b/vi children still went to the two special Dublin schools while adults worked at basket-making at Irish Blindcraft or in telephony jobs around the Dublin-based civil services and banks.

Moving cross-country, one of several action areas was Limerick, where the late Michael Meaney, a talented blind musician and shot-putter who represented Ireland at European Championships in '81 and '83, ensured that the annual Munster Masters Swimming Championships included categories for b/vi participants of all ages.

Rita Rodgers was a key driver of those early organised local, national and international activities. With little sporting background, Rita took to tandem cycling. In 1985 she cycled a tandem down the Champs-Elysées in a prologue to the Grand Finale of the Tour de France. She was the first b/vi woman to cross the line.

15. **The wind beneath our wings**

Pat Kelly (Louth/Limerick), including athletics and tandem cycling.

Pat Kelly was a child sports star, a triple Paralympian and a pioneer of sport for b/vi people in Ireland.

Pat is the reason I took to competitive athletics. His constant persuasive calls suggesting I move from leisure running to track competition won me over. Many of my contemporaries tell a similar story.

Pat was born in 1953 into a family of ten in Limerick. Along with two other brothers, Noel and Munchin, he was diagnosed at an early age with retinitis pigmentosa (RP), which left him with fluctuating vision.

A natural athlete and perennial winner, Pat says, 'While aware of my natural abilities, I never saw myself as talented. I just loved sport.'

In 1966 Pat was the talk of St Joseph's school following his feats at the annual sports day. 'For the long jump, they dug out a 15-foot-long muck pit,' he remembers. 'They put a mat in front of the pit, and I took a run and a jump and landed beyond the pit. My teacher, Fr Murphy, was gobsmacked and brought several priests along for the replay. They moved the mat further back, and I extended my jump.'

Pat had daytime partial sight with no night-time and no indoor vision. In the sports hall he could see nothing but was tops at PE, regularly leading classes and demo-ing exercise positions. But when it came to indoor contact sports, such as futsal or crab football, Pat was lost.

When he heard of an international competition for b/vi people in 1978, he was determined to be first on board.

'A few of the lads with poor vision and myself went to St Joseph's to practise on their running track. This training usually occurred in the late evening, and we had difficulty seeing and staying on the track. I had a brainwave. In my then job in film development at Kodak, they had hundreds of photograph negatives that were being discarded. I took these and laid them down with the white side upwards and formed a white line along the length of the track. We walked the line; we ran the line.'

In 1980, in Arnhem in the Netherlands, Pat, along with Martin Kelly, became Ireland's first b/vi Paralympians.

Pat and his fluctuating eyesight cost him a Paralympic gold medal. Going against the advice of the eyesight classifiers, Pat ran in the B category for partially sighted athletes as opposed to class A for those who were totally blind/no useful vision. His B 400m time of 56.12 was two seconds faster than that achieved in the A final. From gold to dust in two seconds.

Within a year Pat accepted the advice of classifiers, and he ran in the category for totally blind athletes. However, he preferred to run on the outside of his guide runner. Taking the outside lane is uneconomical as runners lose approximately 6 metres per lap, equivalent to 1.5 per cent in time measurement. So Pat was losing a second at 400m and 3.5 seconds at 1500m. Good job he didn't run the 10,000m. (In 1983 IBSA introduced a much tighter classification system where athletics could separate categories for B1, B2 and B3.)

Pat subsequently went on to win double bronze in the 1984 New York Paralympics at 800m and 1500m. He represented Ireland at Barcelona '92 and competed at a World and four European championships. At European level he took 1500m silver in Rome '85 and 400m bronze in Fulda '81.

Pat interrupted his athletics winning streak in 1988 to study and become the first blind person in Ireland to achieve a City & Guilds in Cycling Mechanics at Queen Alexandra College, Birmingham.

From athletics, Pat retired to daily gym exercise routines and open regional and national indoor rowing competitions.

Twenty-five years ago, Pat began tandem cycling the world with Vision Ireland's Blazing Saddles fundraising team. In recent years, he kept it local, taking the Mizen to Malin, bottom to top of Ireland, route with Irish Guide Dogs.

Pat has many happy memories of his times from Mizen to Malin. On his first trip in 1988, he met his wife-to-be, Frances. On his fourteenth and most recent trip in 2022, he had to stop due to heart-related health issues while travelling through Farranfore. He then spent some time recovering at Cork University Hospital.

Pat made a successful full recovery and is now back to his regular routine of cycling and gym work.

'Looking back, I could have taken earlier action. A few weeks before Mizen–Malin, I experienced discomfort around the chest area. I ignored the symptoms, assuming it was indigestion. I advise everyone, especially people of older age, to be aware of, monitor and listen to their body. Don't hesitate to contact medics. Coronary blockages are not just the preserve of the unhealthy, they can happen to anybody, anywhere. Your best insurance is to keep healthy and fit and follow medical guidance. I also found good advice on the Healthy Ireland and the HSE websites, to name two. Never wait until the horse has bolted.'

A day after the Farranfore exit, Pat's first grandchild, Dáire, was born to Alex and Caolán, Pat's son.

In November 2015 Pat Kelly was inducted into the Vision Sports Ireland Hall of Fame.

16. Money's too tight to mention

Fundraising frolics featuring Gay Byrne, Eamonn Coghlan and Eamon Dunphy.

With less than a year to go to our second Paralympic Games, we didn't have the price of a taxi to the airport, never mind our airfare to the USA. Time then for world champion athlete Eamonn Coghlan and his number-one fan Mick Kelly – Pat Kelly's late father – to turn a running vest into gold.

I was out in the infield as Eamonn Coghlan ran a blistering 3.53.48 mile in Dublin in July 1983.

It was a calm, dry Saturday afternoon at the Donore Harriers Coca-Cola International Athletics Meet at UCD, Belfield. As a member of the organising club, I was given a small job on the inside track supporting athletes.

Eamonn Coghlan was in great form that day. He had come off a fantastic indoor season with a new world 3.49.78 mile record.

So, being in the right place at the right time was all-important.

Moments after crossing the line, Eamonn met the media and gargled some Coke for the photographers (he spat it out as soon as the cameras were turned off). As he was exiting along the track area, he exchanged some banter with a group of us from Donore Harriers. I cheekily asked if I could have his shirt to raise some money for b/vi athletes preparing for the Paralympics. 'Of course,' he replied. 'Ring me in a few days as I need to have it washed, it's yours!'

Three days later, I rang Eamonn from an old phone box at the CIE Coldcutt Club in Ballyfermot. 'Where are you, Joe?' When I told him I was at a fundraising function, Eamonn said, 'I'll be right down. Let's present it now.'

I was unprepared – no media, no cameras – so I asked Eamonn to hold off. He reluctantly agreed. We never did have the presentation, as he soon returned to New York. By the time we arrived in New York for the Paralympics, he had returned home to Dublin.

I collected the signed shirt from Eamonn's mother's house on Cooley Road, Drimnagh, and promptly passed it to Mick Kelly.

Mick framed the shirt and organised a raffle around the pubs of Limerick.

Taking the shirt off his back paid immediate dividends as Eamonn Coghlan won the 5,000m at the inaugural World Athletics Championships in Helsinki a month later.

Mick loved the Coghlan shirt, but soon they parted company as his raffle raised a staggering £3,000, €12,000 in current currency.

Mick Kelly, rugby, boxing and athletics lover and our ever-present travelling fan, passed away at age eighty-two in March 1998.

In 1980s Ireland, money was too tight to mention to a government minister with an economy in nosedive. So, it was up to athletes and friends to find funds. We raised money via the traditional route of gigs and sponsored events. A novel Dublin-Dundalk Celebrity Tandem Cycle organised by Pat Kelly, the late John Newman at the Dundalk end, and yours truly at the Dublin end, gained significant publicity and bread in the jar.

Various celebrities piloted tandems a few miles out of Dublin and a few miles into Dundalk in April 1984. The real work was done by the experienced pilots and stokers who took the tandems for most of the 80k back-roads route.

Theresa Mannion ('Don't make unnecessary journeys!'), Jim Sherwin, Tina, Aenghus McAnally, Susan McCann, as well as a variety of politicians and media heads took to the saddle. Among the media participants were *Sunday World* editor Kevin Marron and *Evening Herald* social diarist John Feeney. Seven months later, both died tragically in a plane crash over Eastbourne, England.

On the lighter side, there's always one, Eamon Dunphy. It was a good cycling fall, not a great fall! Paddy Agnew, then sports editor of the *Sunday Tribune*, put Eamo up to it.

I called in to see Paddy before Easter 1984 at his Baggot Street office. 'Paddy,' says I, 'Any chance you could join some fellow journos, some showbiz heads and a few politicos for the start of a tandem cycle involving Ireland's b/vi sportspeople?'

Paddy, feet on desk, thought for a second and beckoned Dunphy (then a *Tribune* writer). 'Yeh, okay, I'll do it,' says Eamo, 'but I haven't cycled a bike since I was ten.'

Fair play to Dunphy, as a few weeks later, he turned up for the ride. There were none of these hi-vis vests, helmets, or reflectors then. He went straight at it and piloted a tandem bicycle accompanied by partially-sighted stoker Philip Dunne.

Legendary broadcaster Michael O'Hehir put Eamon and about twenty other celebs under starter's orders at Dublin's GPO.

They're off! Well, Eamon was off as he wobbled for about 50 metres until he got to the Parnell statue. Then, crash, bang, wallop, off the bike and poor Eamo landed flat on his ass. Nobody was hurt.

However, the then-*Irish Press* editor Tim Pat Coogan was piloting another tandem close by and loved it all. He had great fun teasing Eamo in his print column a week later.

Oh, and on our golden return from New York, we had lots of silver and bronze coins to count, too. Between all funding ventures, including a cheque from the beleaguered government, we raised close to a quarter of a million in today's currency.

Now, that was a great haul, not a good haul, Eamo.

Then, there was our earlier 'haul' of fame …

When thieves decked our haul forty-two Christmases ago, it was a classic case of losers taking it all. The story of our stolen Christmas hamper made national headlines.

Our idea was to raffle a hamper to raise desperately needed funds for our then-governing body at the League. But disaster struck, as thieves stole our hamper. But could we rise and recover, phoenix-like? You bet we could!

The late Gay Byrne said it was the meanest Christmas deed he had ever heard of. Our then-governing body said we brought them into disrepute. Cynics said it was a typical stroke on our part, led by yours truly.

Gay Byrne was the only one who was right, of course.

It began with a brainwave from one of our members: Let's put a hamper together, flog tickets for it on Dublin's Henry Street and raise a tidy sum from the raffle. There would be no costs as all hamper contents could be donated. Sure, we couldn't lose.

The fun began when we started to call local shops for product donations to fill the hamper. I ended up with a few pairs of socks, gloves, and some underwear – most unfestive!

Irish Blindcraft donated a high-quality handmade basket for our low-quality hamper contents.

Christmas time in Henry Street was not to work out. The local casual traders were unimpressed and ran us out of town. There was no space on their patch. Arnott's department store showed the Christmas spirit and gave us a spot under their canopy, but we were now hidden.

Looking back, it should not have been a surprise, but very few people wished to stop to buy our raffle tickets. Those who did suggested we use open buckets and just take donations.

The weeks passed, and our fundraising was a disaster. It couldn't get worse, could it?

I was hardly in the door of my workplace on that December Wednesday morning when our panic-stricken hamper custodian crashed through the same door. 'The hamper was stolen from my van last night. We're wiped out.' Those effin' losers took it all!

To this day, I'm unsure if I even stopped to sympathise with our shocked member. My head was spinning in another direction. Let's share this rotten Christmas bad-luck story with the media and see what happens.

I rang Pat Leahy, then producer of RTÉ Radio's *Listen and See*, the programme 'for and about the blind'. Pat was on the case immediately. On hanging up the phone, he walked out of his office and bumped into Gay Byrne. Gaybo was about to go on air with his number-one radio show and immediately agreed to spread the word, then told his hundreds of thousands of listeners about the mean festive season deed done on blind sports people.

Pat Leahy and RTÉ Radio presenter Robbie Irwin told everyone in the RTÉ radio centre about our hard luck. On air, Larry Gogan, Ronan Collins and Mike Murphy, among others, told listeners our sorry tale.

Donations and goodies came flooding in. Our member, the late Willie Britton, went for it. He rang the top shops and related the story as told by Gay Byrne and his colleagues earlier. More goodies and donations!

Next morning, Thursday, we had turned defeat into victory. Now we had a brand-new hamper with real Christmas goodies. By Thursday evening, we were back out selling raffle tickets for the hamper, with several stores offering us attractive indoor spaces to sell our tickets.

The raffle went ahead that Saturday night and was a major success, raising a brilliant £2,500, €10,000 in today's currency.

Had we really pulled a stroke? No.

Did we bring our then-governing body into disrepute? Their board passed a motion to say we did. Privately, most board members were impressed.

Maybe there's a moral here somewhere: No matter how bad your ideas are, keep the faith, work hard, be honest, and you may just get that lucky break.

17. I only want to tee with you

Ian Corr (Dublin) and Jimmy Murray (Kilkenny), featuring blind golf.

'If there was one good thing about going blind, it was meeting Jimmy Murray,' Ian Corr told me when we met up.

Ian lost his sight through glaucoma following his retirement as head of RTÉ Radio Sport in 2001. He had invited me to drop over to his south Dublin home for a chat about his good friend, the late Jimmy Murray. Jimmy, with wife Maureen, pioneered blind golf in Ireland.

Ian told me, 'Jimmy was a gentleman and the true conscience of Irish Blind Golf.'

He recalled first meeting Jimmy more than twenty years ago, 'My sight began to go, and my great friend Paddy Higgins asked me what could I see. I said I could see my shoes. Paddy said, "In that case, you can see a white golf ball. You can still play golf then."

'We headed out to the Dublin Spawell driving range, where the fella at the desk said, "There's one of your guys out there. His name is Jimmy Murray." We introduced ourselves to each other. Jimmy said he was practising for an Irish Blind Golf Society outing.

'I had spent my life in sport, but never knew there was organised blind golf, although I knew of other organised blind sports. Jimmy signed me up, and Paddy became my guide for the next nine years or so. At one stage, they made me Irish Blind Golf Society captain.'

In a 2023 survey conducted by DCU in association with Vision Ireland and Vision Sports Ireland, an impressive 9.1 per cent of 345 respondents chose blind golf as a favourite activity.

Blind golf is played by totally blind and partially-sighted players with minor modifications to standard rules. The player has a guide who describes distance, direction and characteristics of the green and the location of the hole. The guide may support golf club alignment behind the ball prior to the stroke. From that point, the golfer is on their own. Also, players are permitted to ground their club in a hazard.

Eyesight classifications for blind golf rely solely on visual acuity and do not require field vision measurements for competition. Participants may play in category B1 for totally blind players or in categories B2/B3 for those with a little vision.

The Ripley's Believe It or Not! franchise sponsored the first international blind golf challenge in Minnesota in 1938. Hometown boy Clint Russell defeated the pride of London, Dr William 'Beach' Oxenham. Fifty years later, the International Blind Golf Association was formed. It currently has over 400 registered members from sixteen countries.

Jimmy Murray had partial sight with albinism, an inherited condition that impacts sight where the pigment, which gives hair, skin, and eyes their colour, is missing. As a child, he was a talented athlete who won his first major award in athletics at the Kilkenny School Sports in 1952 over 100 yards. He returned to sprinting thirty years later at our May Games and won more sprint and field accolades.

At blind golf he represented Ireland for two decades at world and other international championships – his medal cabinet overflows.

In 1989 Jimmy became the first chairperson of Vision Sports Ireland. Along with his wife, Maureen, they founded Irish Blind Golf two years later.

Between 1995 and 2000 Jimmy Murray teamed up with John O'Reilly, then caddy to Pádraig Harrington, and organised an annual charity challenge at the Spawell. Jimmy's Irish Blind Golf players competed against the world's top professional golfers – all of whom were blindfolded – including Pádraig Harrington, Colm Montgomerie, Lee Westwood, Seve Ballesteros, Sergio Garcia and Bernhard Langer.

While the results from those challenges have long been shredded, Ian Corr reckons Jimmy Murray would have beaten them all, 'Yeh, Jimmy was very competitive. Paddy and I would meet him for a game of golf in the Spawell most Mondays. He liked to win, and being a Kilkenny man, he mostly did.'

Before he hooked up with Jimmy, Ian Corr was a senior player in RTÉ Radio. 'I was recruited as a technician when television was about to start here in 1960. I ended up on the radio operations side working with Terry Wogan, Larry Gogan and Gay Byrne.'

Ten years later Ian moved to radio sports as a senior producer and worked with Jimmy Magee, Liam Nolan and Philip Greene, among others. A decade on, he became the radio sports boss.

Ian loved his forty years at RTÉ. 'I could count on the fingers on one hand the days I didn't look forward to going in to work. A colleague once told me he would love to be a radio operator for a year – it's like a university where you can study in any department. You could start your day on *Morning Ireland*, move on to religion and farming, and end your shift with sport, learning so much, meeting fascinating people.'

Ian's friend Jimmy Murray loved radio but starred on TV. In 2008 he was featured in the RTÉ series *This Is Me*. The episode was called 'Teeing Is Believing', where viewers saw Jimmy at home with Maureen and on the course at the Spawell.

The last time I saw Jimmy Murray was in October 2016, and it was special. As the then-chair of Vision Sports Ireland, I embarked on a mission, almost impossible. The boys of Irish Blind Golf laid the trap. I was to turn up unannounced at the Hermitage golf clubhouse in Lucan, Co. Dublin. Jimmy would be there, but I was to lie low.

The moment arrived, and I was invited to the podium. I was honoured to induct Jimmy Murray into the Vision Sports Ireland Hall of Fame. Jimmy was floored but not lost for words. Irish Blind Golf members gave him a standing ovation.

Some months later I learned Jimmy was unwell. To our loss, he passed away peacefully on 19 December 2018. At his funeral, we learned that he was so proud of his Hall of Fame award that it held centre place on his mantlepiece.

18. My mama always told me there'd be mays like this

May games/Mayfest 1981 – present.

Saturday, 2 May 1981 was the day we launched Mayfest, the May Games. Over five decades, the games have proven to be the springboard into sport for thousands of b/vi people in Ireland.

On Sunday, 2 May 2021 it was quite the honour to co-host, with ex-Vision Sports Ireland director Bernie Everard, the opening ceremony for the 40th anniversary Mayfest. Due to the Covid-19 pandemic, it was a virtual ceremony. Many involved in those first games popped up on screen for our anniversary. Oh, what a night.

The Mayfest story began on 7 September 1980 as we returned by boat from Stranraer to Larne. We had just competed at Coatbridge Stadium, Glasgow, where I had won my first b/vi race at 1500m. As the resident typewriter person, I was given two jobs, both of which resulted in historic outcomes.

Firstly, word was out that the inaugural European Games for the Blind would take place in West Germany the following year. Could I suss it out? Our newly formed club had no money and was unlikely to support submitting an Irish entry. I wrote to the organisers, who replied that they would welcome us with open arms.

Secondly, we were aware at the time that we were the ultimate party crashers. We were at everyone's party – at games across

Skiing is believing – Gus and Paula Dorrington (centre) supported by Eddie (left) and Kathleen Sythes (right). Photo: Vision Ireland Insight.

Hoops of joy with Freya Reaper. Photo: Vision Sports Ireland.

Blind and vision-impaired ladies have been rowing our rivers for over a century. Here rowers are vying for places for London 2012. Photo: Vision Ireland Insight.

Des Kenny trolley raced and played crab football and chess at St Joseph's School for Blind Boys in Drumcondra. He was CEO of Vision Ireland from 1986 to 2014. Photo: Vision Ireland Insight.

In 2014 Jimmy Gallagher (left) was awarded the Vision Sports Ireland Hall of Fame by Chairperson Robert Dobbyn (right). Photo: Karl Leonard.

After a tactical tandem road race Katie-George Dunlevy and Eve McCrystal win gold in Tokyo 2020, their third Paralympic gold medal. Photo: Sportsfile.

In 2014 Frank Cullinan (left) was awarded the Vision Sports Ireland Hall of Fame by Vision Sports Ireland Chairperson Robert Dobbyn (right). Photo: Karl Leonard.

The long way home. Triple Paralympian and double medallist Pat Kelly races outside his guide Eoin Reddin, Morton Stadium, 1984. Most blind athletes choose to run inside their guide to save valuable seconds on a curved running track. Photo: Pat Kelly.

Left to right: World 5000m champion Eamonn Coughlan, Vision Sports Ireland Chairperson Robert Dobbyn, Paralympic superstar Jason Smyth and future Taoiseach Leo Varadkar. It was thumbs up for the rebrand of Irish Blind Sports to Vision Sports Ireland, September 2013. Photo: Vision Sports Ireland.

Jimmy Murray, first chairperson of Vision Sports Ireland and founder of Irish Blind Golf. Photo: Vision Ireland Insight.

Carol Carr, winner of the B2 400m at the 1984 Paralympic Games in New York, Ireland's first ever gold medal in the blind/vi category at the Paralympic Games. Photo: Joe Geraghty.

Sean McDowell (right) Ireland vi rugby captain with coach, team manager and former Italy fly half Ian Mc Kinley. Photo: Vision Sports Ireland.

Audrey Darby, ChildVision Equestrian Centre, with her young pupil as she familiarises herself with a pony. Photo: Audrey Darby

Bridie Lynch was Ireland's sole gold medal winner at the 1996 Paralympic Games in Atlanta when she won at the B3 discus. She subsequently was awarded the Vision Sports Ireland Hall of Fame and the inaugural Paralympics Ireland Hall of Fame. Photo: Sportsfile.

Francis H. Merrick created the adapted tactile braille chess board in 1902. Eighty-seven years later, Ireland take on Hungary at the IRISZ Kupa (IRIS Cup) in Szentendre in Hungary, 1989. Photo: Philip Doyle.

Jason's first para-race. At Vision Sports Ireland Mayfest 2005 Jason Smyth wins the 100m to qualify for the IPC European Para-athletics Championships in Espoo, Finland. Three months later in Finland Jason wins the first of his twenty-one championship gold medals. Photo: Vision Ireland Insight.

the UK – but never hosted our own. I wrote a letter to our club, making the case to host our own games.

Both our sports club and its overlords, the League board, were keen. 1981 was the International Year of Disabled, and a Dublin Games fitted in perfectly with their aims.

Nine months later, Mayfest was born. 'On yer marks …' Bang!

Even the sun came out for the Saturday afternoon athletics at the new track at the Morton Stadium in Santry, Dublin.

Earlier that historic day, I popped into Dublin's Irish Life Centre for the Irish Swimming Gala for b/vi people. As I entered the swimming pool area, I was greeted with a crescendo of screams from teenage schoolgirls. They were excited by the outstanding performances of their friends, who were breaking records to beat the band.

With a pounding head from the shrieks and whoops, I joined my colleagues on our hired coach: destination, Santry.

We arrived a little behind time to find every top athletics official in Ireland, led by the late Brendan Foreman, present. The then-Irish athletics governing body, Bord Lúthchleas na hÉireann (BLE), had rolled out the red carpet for their contribution to the 1981 International Year of Disabled.

The echo of the starter's gun for the 800m final had a massive impact on Lancaster's Norman Theobald. Norman must have thought he got a bullet up his backside as he went off like the clappers. The rest of us chatted our way over the first few hundred metres. As we ran out of chat, Norman Theobald ran out of oxygen, and I strode away for an Irish record. I did alright that day, as I also won the 1500m.

I recall Des Kenny, cigarette in one hand, microphone in the other, picking me off the line for an interview. Des was freelancing for RTÉ Radio's *Listen & See*.

My 800m win earned me the first athletics gold medal of the very first Mayfest.

In between my races, I watched in utter amazement as sixteen-year-old Carol Carr blew the adult field away at 100m, 200m and 400m. Another teenager, Fintan O'Donnell, smashed long- and high-jump records for fun.

Minister for Sport, the late Jim Tunney TD, was trackside with his chequebook. A grant for Mayfest and a grant for our European Games-bound team, no applications required.

The late Fergus O'Brien, Lord Mayor of Dublin, spoke at the post-Games meal at the old Hollybank Hotel on Dublin's Howth Road. Later, the rest of us took to the disco floor thinking we were Shakin' Stevens.

It was a day, a night, to be forever treasured. And yet, it feels like only yesterday.

Four plus decades later, Mayfest includes the A–Z of sport with a mix of competition and come-and-try activities. Try anything from wrestling to wall-climbing to water sports; from vi rugby to vi tennis to blind golf. The first sports of swimming and athletics are still so popular.

Mayfest is the second-longest-running games of its type in the world, just behind the London Metro Games, which began in 1977 to celebrate Queen Elizabeth's silver jubilee.

The party over after our first Mayfest, we settled into preparing for our first European Games, which took place in August in Fulda, West Germany. Our instant love of the Euros led to us hosting the championships twelve years later.

While 1981 was a historical year for b/vi sports in Ireland, it was also the year of the founding of the International Blind Sports Federation in Paris (IBSA). Ireland is an active IBSA member, and we participated in its World Games in Birmingham in August 2023.

The advent of IBSA, founder members of the International Paralympics Committee (IPC), also added shape and rules to a rapidly growing world b/vi sports movement.

19. **Gold**

Athlete Carol Carr (Dublin).

Teenage sensation Carol Carr blazed a golden trail across the world of b/vi athletics in the 1980s. In four short years, she won five gold medals and a silver at Paralympic and European championships.

Four decades later, Ireland's first b/vi Paralympic gold medallist is circumspect. 'I discovered then that I had a talent for something which gave me confidence, the self-belief and freedom that I wasn't experiencing as a teenager. Until then, I wasn't involved in any extracurricular activities at school or in the community. It brought such a positive number of things into my life that gave me the platform to gather my energy and go forward with a career as a qualified social worker in the UK and Ireland.'

Dubliner Carol was born in December 1964 with an underdeveloped optic nerve, leaving her with no central vision and limited peripheral vision. The eye condition has remained static.

Carol's early athletic talent came to the fore through her daily commutes between St Mary's School for Blind Girls in Merrion, Dublin, where she boarded, and her day school at St Anne's Secondary School in Milltown, Dublin.

'Once the 3.20 pm exit bell rang,' she recalls, 'I took orders from my school pals for toffee logs, brown bags of broken KitKat and suchlike and raced up that quarter-mile hill to the Barn, the local corner shop. I never failed to return laden down with the goodies in time for the 3.30 pm bus back to Merrion.'

The first time Carol ran on an athletics track was for our inaugural Mayfest in 1981. 'That was a very exciting time,' she says. 'Carol Hayes, a visiting athletics expert from IWA Sport, appeared at our school and introduced us to track and field. She told us there was just enough time to get ready for the national b/vi games in Santry, Dublin. I jumped at the chance and trained hard.'

Following triple gold at Mayfest, Carol was selected with me and seven more for our first European Games in Fulda in West Germany later that summer.

In the last race of the last day, Carol Carr won our first-ever international gold.

As I was running in the final of the 3000m, Carol was preparing for the 1500m final. We both warmed up together and finalised our race strategies.

My plan of hanging back worked until the bell. On the back straight, my opponents sprinted out of sight. Goodbye, medals!

Carol's similar strategy worked like a dream. She explains, 'I was by then used to fast one-lap races, but 1500m was different. I was very surprised that I was able to keep up over four laps and still had enough energy to pull away from the leader coming on to the final straight.' Gold!

Two years later, we returned to the Europeans in Varna, Bulgaria. In less than twenty-four hours, Carol won two gold medals and set two world records at 400m and 1500m.

I nicked silver myself at 5000m with an Irish b/vi record, which still stands.

A year later, Carol secured Ireland's first-ever Paralympic gold for b/vi athletes in New York, where she won the 400m. She won silver at 1500m at the same Paralympics.

Carol says, 'My New York preparations had been disrupted by a period of ill health just four months beforehand. Thankfully, I had trained hard before I was ill, and it paid off.

'The 400m race, which gave me gold, is a bit of a blur. But I'll never forget the great surprise as I crossed the line and saw my dad, who appeared from nowhere. I thought he was in Dublin.'

I was in on that plan and assisted Barney Carr, Carol's dad, to get to the inside track. It was fabulous.

As for my own track performance, I reached the final of the 1500m, breaking another Irish record, which still stands, but pulled my Achilles tendon while doing so. Wrapped in a bandage, I ran in the 5000m final, finishing fifth. I still ran the 1500m final the next day, but the Irish team management ordered me off the track after struggling through three of the four laps.

The Irish b/vi team was then ranked in the top ten in Europe and finished fourteenth in the world at the '84 Paralympic Games.

After winning further gold at 1500m at the Rome '85 Europeans, Carol had to prioritise time for education and career. Sadly, she never returned to track racing but continued active sport until a skiing accident twenty years ago. Carol suffered a torn cruciate ligament, which has had an ongoing adverse impact.

When asked to advise up-and-coming youth, Carol says, 'I would encourage each to passionately pursue your dreams, to put in the consistent training, which will enable you to reach your full potential. Most importantly, always remember, it is not just about attaining the gold medals, but about enjoying the journey.'

Carol Carr was inducted into the Vision Sports Ireland Hall of Fame in May 2021, exactly forty years to the day after her first race victory in events for sport for b/vi people.

20. I get a kick out of you

Futsal with player-coach Tony Lyster (Dublin) and vi rugby with captain Sean McDowell (Down). Gaelic games also included.

B/vi players have been on the ball with various adaptations of soccer, rugby and GAA for over a century.

In 1982 soccer kicked in internationally when club teams consisting of partially sighted (B2/B3) players from Manchester, London and Dublin competed at five-a-side in the second annual Mayfest. Subsequently, these tournaments became a Mayfest staple, with Irish teams reciprocating by playing in UK tournaments. Special thanks to Ron Goulden (Northern Sports) and Andrew Kalavazides (Metro Sports), who regularly brought their teams to Dublin and were key to developing the sport here.

At Mayfest 2016 President Michael D. Higgins dropped by to chat with teams from Ireland, the UK and Austria.

In the early years, our teams had minimal structure and limited success. Ireland futsal team manager and goalkeeper Tony Lyster recalls the turning point and the move to regular coaching and training sessions.

'In the early 90s I remember having a meeting with Lar Currid and Henry Randle, both past pupils of St Joseph's in Drumcondra. We began holding weekly training sessions at Trinity College.

'We moved on to having five-a-side kickabouts and friendly matches with the gardaí from Dublin's Harcourt Street station.

For eighteen months they beat us, but then one night, we beat them 13-12. It was like winning the FA Cup!'

I asked Tony if the gardaí arrested them afterwards. 'No, they were delighted for us and joined in the celebrations. That gave us the confidence to kick on and put winning runs together. For three years, our team was unbeaten against all UK opposition.'

By now, our players had progressed to futsal, where minimal rule changes apply. The key difference is that there is a minimum number of B2 players required to be on the pitch at any one time during the game. This game is played using a standard indoor futsal ball – with high visibility being an option when available.

In 1997 the Irish were invited to the European B2/B3 Futsal Championships in Barcelona. With just six weeks and a small squad, 'We got destroyed but learned our lesson,' recalls Tony.

They returned to the Euros four years later and almost pulled off a sensational victory against hosts France. 'We were 1-0 up with 30 seconds to go,' recalls Tony. 'We conceded a corner and lost concentration. We didn't have a player on the post, bang, 1-1. Still, the result was the shock of the tournament. We beat Greece later in that tournament.'

By then the FAI had officially started to cap players, and Vision Sports Ireland supported our B2/B3 Futsal teams to compete with pride in competitions from Brazil to Italy and from Spain to Turkey.

Tony Lyster is very proud of his part in bringing futsal to the next level. He recalls being at Dublin Castle and sitting beside Ireland soccer legend Ray Houghton for the presentation of caps. 'Ray says to me, "This is brilliant, I got my first cap in the post!"'

In 2012 I bumped into former Ireland captain and Lions rugby player Fergus Slattery. He was enthused about disability rugby in the UK and how blind and partially sighted men were participating. I explained how we played tag rugby at St Joseph's in the 1960s.

In November 2021, nine years after meeting the Lions king, during a short respite from Covid, we had our first try at vi rugby here.

Sean McDowell, now captain of the Irish vi rugby team, recalls the first session at Dublin's Old Wesley Club. 'It was the day after my sister Tara's wedding. I was very nervous. My balance was way off due to a serious brain injury fifteen months earlier. My wife, Áine, and brother-in-law, Aidan, held me up as we went through the training drills.'

Sean is from Annalong, near Newcastle in Co. Down. He played soccer with Mourne Rovers up to age twenty-eight and Gaelic football with Glasdrumman until he was thirty-three.

Then came the life-changer. 'Six years ago, I collapsed at home. The scan showed I had arteriovenous malformation (AVM), which impacts blood flow to the brain. They were reluctant to operate here, so I underwent radiotherapy in Sheffield. We thought it was sorted, but on 8 June 2020, while out in my garden, I got the worst pain ever. My sight went, and I was rushed to hospital for emergency surgery.'

After a lengthy spell in hospital, Sean returned home with left-side hemianopia, leaving him with very little vision. He also lost the hearing in his right ear and had poor balance and some memory issues. Consuming food was also difficult. Overcoming the trauma physically and mentally was a challenge that Sean was up for.

'My uncle Paul encouraged me to go to the local hotel gym in the Burrendale Hotel, where I worked with him and my personal trainer, Gina. The first day, I tried the treadmill at 0.5 miles per hour (the slowest setting), and it was too fast for me, but I persisted with their help and within a year, I could run a six-minute mile.'

Sean's speedy recovery was phenomenal. He believes his sporting background was a major help. However, his GAA senior football days were over, and he was on the lookout for alternative low-sight, friendly alternatives.

'When registering with the RNIB, I met their Eye Clinic Liaison Officer who suggested vi rugby, which was at its formative stage in Ireland.'

Vi rugby is based on the rugby sevens touch format. The ball contains bells. In Ireland, male and female players join on the one team. It is governed by the Irish Rugby Football Union (IRFU) with support from Vision Sports Ireland.

Just eighteen months after their first training session, Old Wesley Irish team hosted England's London Harlequins in UCD at Mayfest '23.

The Irish team is coached by David McKay and Dublin-born Italy fly-half Ian McKinley. Thirteen years ago, Ian lost the sight of his left eye in a rugby field accident. Determined to return to the game, he pioneered sports goggles and, against all forces, returned to the game at its highest level.

Of their game against London Harlequins, Sean McDowell says, 'To see where we were at against Harlequins compared to our first day was something else. The joy, the excitement. After my brain injury, I never thought I would play sports again. I'm now looking forward to many more years playing at home and abroad.'

In October 2023 the Old Wesley/Vision Sports team represented Ireland and finished second in the inaugural VI Rugby World Cup in France.

As rugby begins to move through the phases, adapted GAA is about to take to the field. It was trialled at Mayfest '18 and '23. The GAA, in association with Vision Sports Ireland, have been exploring adaptations, including bell balls and large hurleys. Meanwhile, the rule book is being prepared.

In a 2023 survey conducted by DCU in association with Vision Ireland and Vision Sports Ireland, an impressive 7.1 per cent of 345 respondents chose Gaelic football as a favourite activity. All indications are that the rollout of b/vi GAA will be a massive boost to sport in the community, especially within schools and colleges.

Here we go, here we go, here we go ... to Croke Park.

21. Hanging on the telephone

The founding of Vision Sports Ireland.

The 1980s were our glory days, a golden era when all was new. Our journey, which began with a weekend in Falkirk in September 1978, was now criss-crossing several UK cities including London, Manchester, Stoke Mandeville, Peterborough and Glasgow.

It was Saturday night after the competition and the air was getting hot – time to party. At the bar, the banter was about nearly winning the 100m, but now working on the 100 litres! On the dance floor, love stories began (some endured, some ended).

Seoul Paralympian Gus Dorrington fondly remembers early days in Scotland. 'Irish Blindcraft manager Terry McAndrews called us into the boardroom. He said that by going to international athletics in Scotland, we were making history. He gave us two days' paid leave.' Terry, who had albinism, was a gifted musician and actor who was a leading light in b/vi welfare.

Gus was good at the long jump, high jump and low jump. Low jump? Gus explains: 'Yeah, after competition, we went to this Glasgow bar, which was very dark. I headed for the loo but entered through the wrong door. There's a big step, and next thing bump! Bump! Bump! Head over heels into the beer cellar where an Alsatian awaited! Holy f***! I was up those steps quicker than

I went down. As I recovered, two Scottish lads asked me what happened. I told them I forgot my parachute.'

As for the Alsatian, 'He got such a fright he leapt over the bar taking fifty quid's worth of drink with him!'

Our annual Mayfest was the must-attend competition for athletes throughout the British Isles. From 1983 to 1988, the Ireland and Great Britain athletics teams to compete at Paralympic, European and World Games were selected based on results from Mayfest. RTÉ TV, national radio and print media covered our best moments.

The games' dinner dances were the hottest ticket in town. The annual pool competition at Dublin's Baggot Inn was a day and a night to remember.

Over following decades, the May games – I renamed them Mayfest in 2013 – have evolved to keep pace with the changing disability landscape. No matter how much the format changed, they keep attracting participants. Some of the biggest Mayfests were held two decades ago when athletes travelled from across Europe. The 2005 Mayfest, the 25th Anniversary Games, were historic as it was there that Paralympic golden boys Jason Smyth and Michael McKilllop, were 'discovered'. More recently, a record 400 participants attended Mayfest 2023.

Some weekends lasted for days after the official programme closed. As many of our players, including myself, then worked on government switchboards, it was often commented that irate government customers could be left hanging on the telephone on the Monday after Mayfest.

The volume and variety of emerging sports – judo, equestrian, tenpin bowling, tandem cycling and more – were too hot to handle; too hot for the superb trade-union-driven National League of the

Blind. After Seoul '88 came the soul-searching. Change was on the way.

On Saturday, 26 November 1988, at Dublin's North Star Hotel, now the Address Connolly, I joined thirty or so passionate sports enthusiasts as Irish Blind Sports was born. Writer and broadcaster Liam Nolan kept manners on us all as chair. At the time, Liam was the chief executive of the Olympic Council of Ireland. In earlier years, Liam Nolan was a BBC radio boxing and athletics commentator who crossed over to radio prime-time current affairs. He also worked with ITV before moving home to Ireland in the late 1960s.

From RTÉ's Henry Steet studios, Liam hosted a daily programme, *The Liam Nolan Hour*, which lasted almost two hours. Liam's daily show was the first personality-driven programme of its kind in Ireland and set the stage for Gay Byrne, Pat Kenny, Claire Byrne and many others. Liam had a keen interest in disability sports, and his son, also Liam, went on to compete at Special Olympics.

Meanwhile, back at the North Star, we joined Liam and his brother John as we formed an eleven-member steering committee. Within six months, Irish Blind Sports, rebranded as Vision Sports Ireland in 2013, was a not-for-profit company limited by guarantee and a registered charity recognised by all required national and world sports governing bodies.

Athletes from Northern Ireland could choose between the new Dublin-based governing body or remaining with the London-based British Blind Sports (BBS). BBS was founded twelve years earlier and works hand in glove with Vision Sports Ireland. Both are members of IBSA. In more recent years Disability Sport Northern Ireland have provided all with invaluable support.

Keeping all sports running was seamless, although we hadn't a penny in our new bank account. With a little help from our friends as well as an income-gathering life membership scheme, we hosted a very successful 1989 May festival of sport.

We celebrated our fifth birthday in 1993 by hosting the world's biggest sports event of the year for b/vi sports people.

Liam Nolan became our first president in 1989, a role he performed until 2003. He retired from broadcasting in the mid-1990s as his hearing deteriorated. Since then, he has been a very successful author.

Liam's friend, former boss and eminent rugby commentator Fred Cogley replaced him as president. Fred served for six very successful years and attended all the major events. In mid-twentieth-century Ireland, Fred was to rugby what Michael O'Hehir was to GAA: 'the Voice'.

In 2009 Colm Murray, the voice of newsreading, horse-racing and Paralympic Games, took over our presidential reigns. Within months Colm was diagnosed with motor neurone disease but bravely continued to serve until his death in July 2013.

22. I will walk 500 miles

Walking and trekking with Theresa Lavin (Meath) and Michael Lavin (Roscommon).

Michael and Theresa Lavin are top of the table down at the League of the Blind on Dublin's Hill Street. When not guiding the League's executive board, they are stepping it out and leading organised walks for b/vi people across Ireland's east coast and beyond.

Recently, I trekked to the League's HQ for a walk down memory lane with Michael and Theresa.

'We began the walks about forty years ago,' Michael recalls. 'It was the late Ollie Mooney, Chair of the League for many years, who led the way. Joe Dodd, our minibus driver, would take us out to a scenic area and off we'd go.'

Soon, a structure and walks pattern emerged. Theresa recalls, 'I worked at Trinity College, where we had a great network. My colleague Ana Reilly got her friends and neighbours to join us as guides. Each year, from April to September, we met up for three- to-seven-mile walks followed by refreshments in a local hostelry. On maybe one Saturday each month, we might head a little further out.'

'Over the years, guides have always been hard to find,' says Michael. 'We are so grateful for all the support we receive from groups such as An Óige.'

Michael, from Boyle, Co. Roscommon, was born with keratoconus, which is a weakening of the centre of the cornea, which eventually led to total loss of sight. Theresa is from Kilcloon in Co. Meath. She was born two months premature and has the Stevie Wonder condition of *retinopathy of prematurity* (ROP).

Michael and Theresa were not active sportspeople at school. 'But the slow bicycle races were great crack,' says Michael. 'At St Mary's College in Boyle, we were mad about bikes. We could do magic, but the slow bicycle race over twenty minutes was the biggest challenge.'

Michael's cycling skills were to return with a bang a decade after leaving school.

'Theresa and I had a very good friend, Catherine Waldron. We asked her if she would come out for a cycle. She had never been on a tandem, but off we went, herself and me. At Cross Guns Bridge in Glasnevin, Dublin, we took a sharp turn left and clipped the kerb. We fell on top of each other and laughed it off.

'A month later, just before we married, I brought Theresa to meet my landlord. "Oh," he says, "So that woman you were lying on top of at Cross Guns wasn't your wife then?"' It may be that Michael advised his landlord to take a hike.

Michael and Theresa have hiked to Mount Brandon in Kerry and further afield with their walking group to Salzburg and Prague. In 2023 Vision Ireland organised the Vision Walk in association with Marbella Four Days Walking, covering distances of up to 30 km a day.

Successive member surveys over the past forty years have placed walking among the top three leisure activities for b/vi people. Indeed, it is number one in recent research from the 'Visibility for Women in Sport' Stage Two research project, which was conducted by DCU in partnership with Vision Sports Ireland and Vision Ireland. It found that 100 per cent of a small sample of b/vi interviewees chose walking as their primary form of exercise. As much as 88 per cent had engaged in a recreational walk in the past week, compared to a national average of 66 per cent (Irish Sports Monitor, 2022).

Aside from leisure walking, many like the great adventure. The Terracotta Ramblers were founded in 1993 to promote health, fitness and funding support for Vision Ireland and the Richmond Brain Research Foundation. Project management was led by Eamon Duffy (Vision Ireland) and Mary Quinn (Richmond).

From the Grand Canyon to the Great Wall of China, Argentina to New Zealand, and Peru to Malaysia, they hiked 20–35 km a day. Groups of up to 120 joined the expedition, including b/vi participants Robert Dowdall and Gus and Paula Dorrington. The peak of their success was climbing to base camp and above, on Mount Everest.

The most recent b/vi climber to reach Everest Base Camp was Jennifer Doherty from Buncrana in Donegal. In 2004 Jennifer and her family fled the tsunami in Thailand as waves encircled them. It was a life-changing experience for the young b/vi girl who resolved never to let her disability stop her from achieving. With support from the Donegal Centre for Independent Living, Jennifer went on top of the world in May 2022.

Of the many Irish blind adventurers, Mark Pollock, from Holywood, Co. Down, is one remarkable sportsman. In 2009, after a 43-day expedition, he became the first blind person to reach the South Pole. Mark is simply poles apart from the rest of us.

Away from snow and ice, it's the wind and rain for our League walking group, now led by Veronica Coffey. Kathleen and Nora Doyle also organise Thursday afternoon walks in the Dublin area from March to November.

The Cork Visually Impaired Walking Group was founded in 2008 by Vision Ireland's Niamh Connolly and Anne Maria Hennessy. With support from Cork Local Sports Partnership and Vision Sports Ireland, they criss-cross Cork's beauty spots on alternate Saturdays through most of the year.

The stepping stones to success were laid by the late Hilary Dornan, Pat Walsh, Paul Droney, Geraldine Looney and Derry Walsh, to name a few.

The Galway Visually Impaired Activity Club was founded in May 2006. They encourage members to participate in all sports and organise walks and tandem cycles, both locally, cross-country and cross-continent.

The RNIB NI Community Connection Programme has a comprehensive list of daily activities across the region, including walking, boccia, vi tennis and golf. RNIB invite you to connect with others who are blind or partially sighted to share interests and experiences and support each other.

Once a year, b/vi people meet up for a weekend of walking, talking, dancing, romancing, pints and paninis. Michael Sutton arranged such weekends for many years at various country locations. For the past fifteen years, Pat Kelly and Maureen Madden have taken on the mantle with cross-border long and short strolls each June.

On the benefits of walking, both Michael and Theresa Lavin agree: 'As members of the older community, walking has helped us feel healthier and fitter. We have been to so many places and have had a real insight into Dublin city. We have the confidence to enjoy the great outdoors.'

True, all you need is the air that you breathe and walking.

23. Ride on

Equine therapy with ChildVision occupational therapy manager Audrey Darby (Dublin).

Fifty years later, I'm back at St Joseph's.

The old main entrance has moved up the road. There's a new nameplate, *ChildVision National Education Centre for Blind Children*.

Our running track and football field of dreams are both sold for private home construction. Beyond the old castle and church, there's a wonderful all-weather children's playground. It's safe to say they can't push the swings 180 degrees and jump from 6ft high into cutting gravel, as we did.

The old assembly hall, our ballroom of first romance, is now multi-purpose and extends into Jojo's café.

A stroll onto Jojo's veranda is a walk into the country in the city. A beautifully landscaped, accessible series of walkways leads to the ChildVision Equine Centre. This area was a farm where I spent my Mays picking spuds and Septembers collecting conkers and raiding its apple house.

On a sunlit October morning, I sit for coffee on Jojo's veranda with Audrey Darby, who for nineteen years has been ChildVision's Occupational Therapy Manager and now devotes all her skills and efforts to the equine centre.

The ChildVision Equine Centre is a world leader in promoting the use of horses and equine-related activities to achieve therapeutic goals such as enhancing physical, emotional, social, cognitive, behavioural, and educational skills for people with disabilities.

Audrey tells the story, 'We started to build the equine therapy service about thirteen years ago. At that point, we had existing stables and an instructor who brought her horse with her for weekly sessions. We started tentatively with pre-school children and were amazed at how they progressed.

'Brian Allen, our then CEO, had great vision. He brought in the staff and the resources we needed to set up the unit, and over time, it grew and developed. Terri Brosnan joined as Equine Therapy Manager in 2016, and I joined full-time in 2017. Since then, the unit has gone from strength to strength and developed to provide equine-assisted occupational therapy (EAOT) and equine-assisted therapy (EAT) services to children and young adults with blindness.'

So, how can b/vi children benefit from equine therapy?

Audrey explains: 'We each have seven sensory systems: touch, taste, sight, hearing, smell and body awareness (also known as the proprioceptive sense). Finally, there's movement and balance, based in your ears. The ears are very closely connected with the eyes and one's balance. All these systems work through the cerebellum in the back of the brain. Consequently, mobility, vision and hearing are all connected. So, if you take away vision, your balance is affected.

'If you place a baby with little or no vision on their tummy on the floor, they'll just lie there because they have no stimulus. If they could see, they would lift their head and push up. They would think, *Oh, what's that?* They'll push into sitting, they'll push into moving, they'll crawl to get to it, to touch it, to feel it. The driving factor is vision. Without vision, the child will be more passive, which affects how their motor co-ordination develops. It can affect their ability to do sports later and their ability to co-ordinate themselves in space to be able to do orientation and mobility.

'Horses can help lay foundations. A horse has incredible movement. It's one of only three species with a specific movement of the pelvis: humans, horses and pigs, but we're not going to ride pigs.

'When you put a child onto a horse, and the horse moves, the movement of the human pelvis mirrors that of the horse in response to that movement. Their body must work to remain balanced and co-ordinates the contraction and relaxation of all the muscles of the trunk to respond to that movement. The effect is infinitely better and more therapeutic than putting them on a static therapy ball.

'By stimulating the sensory systems by moving in specific ways when on the horse, we can help mature the body's responses. This helps with motor co-ordination, spatial awareness, balance, reacting to and understanding more about the world as we experience it. This is especially important to those children who do not tend to actively seek out enough movement to help these processes happen innately through everyday activities.'

While ideally the horse is the therapeutic medium, Audrey and the team first conduct full assessments, which should end with a meeting between child and animal.

Audrey continues: 'For a blind person, the horse can be very scary. We spend a lot of time working around the concepts. Like, what is a horse? Where are his legs? Can you feel his legs? Here's his tail. We must have a calm horse as the child might step on a hoof. You may have the child's parents and guardians with them for the initial stages on the horse, but then they step back a little to facilitate the child's independence. Parents and guardians will, however, remain involved at all stages as therapeutic input progresses.'

The ChildVision Equine Centre brings out the best in its students. Audrey tells me of one beautiful shy girl. 'She has gone from being withdrawn, having poor balance and mobility, to come out of herself and make new friends, to learning writing skills and becoming more of a leader in the group. She's learning a sport which is giving her social engagement. The difference that this has made for her is phenomenal.

'It is extremely rare that students who come to the equine therapy centre do not grow to love the horses. While most start by engaging in a therapeutic process through being on the horse, several students have progressed to carrying out stable management, and some have even used skills learnt in this area to open work opportunities.'

Historically, b/vi people have engaged in equine sport, and even enjoyed the extremely dangerous hunt over the past few centuries. B/vi people on farms have also befriended horses.

Dressage is the ideal competitive sport of choice. Two b/vi dressage riders, Joan Salmon (Atlanta and Sydney) and Ann Harvey (Sydney), represented Ireland at the Paralympic Games. Classification for Paralympic Games is complex. The B3 partially sighted rider is ineligible. B1 competitors join in the merged Grade IV, with athletes with different physical disabilities B2 riders compete in Grade V, also against athletes with different disabilities.

Doug Stevenson won the Novice and Under-24 categories at the (able-bodied) Irish National Dressage Championships and then went on to represent his country internationally.

At the ChildVision Equine Centre, Audrey Darby and the team provide therapeutic input to support skill development for b/vi people from childhood to young adulthood, from early development to lifelong learning. Older students attend and develop at physical, sensory and psychosocial levels.

The bond between the b/vi rider and their horse means no fence is too high.

24. Simply the best

Athlete Bridie Lynch (Donegal).

'In life, we have the highs, the lows, the good, the bad and the ugly. I've been lucky to have one constant in life: sport. Sport is in my blood.'

Bridie Lynch understands the agonies and ecstasies more than most. From Ireland's golden girl at Atlanta 1996 to elimination in Sydney 2000, where she broke her foot with her discus, she has celebrated national awards, including the 1996 Person of the Year, and then endured family tragedy combined with ill health.

I caught up with Bridie in central Dublin on her fifty-seventh birthday. She looks every bit the star athlete she was and still is.

Bridie, from St Johnston in Co. Donegal, was born with Hermansky-Pudlak syndrome, which features albinism. 'Hermansky is a rare blood disorder, and not many people realise how serious it is,' Bridie explains. 'It has triggered several health issues for me over the years, leading to serious blood loss and the inflammatory bowel condition of Crohn's disease.'

In seventeen years Bridie won thirty-four World- and European-class medals. She made her debut at the 1983 European Games for the Blind in Varna, Bulgaria, where she won bronze in the discus.

When we chat about Bulgaria, Bridie shrieks in horror, recalling the homebound flight. 'I didn't think it would ever get into the sky; the plane had propellors. It was a banger, and I thought it would crash.'

A smoother flight path lay ahead for Bridie with her first Paralympic Games in 1984 in New York, where she was a discus and shot-put finalist. Two years later Bridie won double silver at the inaugural World Championships in Gothenburg. Her first gold, in discus, arrived at the Euros in Moscow in 1987.

Bridie was among the favourites to win gold in Seoul '88, but her discus event was dramatically pulled at the last minute. 'Ouch, I was disappointed, but I had to get over it to compete again.'

She returned to the Paralympics in 1992 in Barcelona, where she won double silver in the discus and pentathlon (five sports: 100m, 800m, discus, shot-put and long jump).

1996 was Bridie's year. In February she became the first Irish person with a disability to win a national mainstream athletics title. At Nenagh, in the shot-put, she won the BLE National Indoor Championships. 'It all changed when coach Eamonn Harvey took care of me. My distances improved dramatically, and I shot-put over 12 metres at Nenagh and later over 42 metres for discus in Belfield.

'At Atlanta '96 I was up against the Russians, an unknown entity, but it all happened on the day. So hot, so humid, but I got that fantastic discus throw.'

Bridie was Ireland's only Paralympic gold medal winner at Atlanta '96 and returned to a rapturous reception nationwide.

'People say London 2012 changed our views on disability. I'd say '96 was a game-changer here in Ireland. I returned to receive a People of the Year Award, I faced Pat Kenny on the *Late Late*, and I received numerous awards, including the Freedom of Donegal.

'Until then, people confused Paralympics and Special Olympics. They still do it, but not like they used to. Physical and intellectual must always be separated and understood. While mine is physical, I understand intellectual, as most of us are learning to understand.'

Like all Irish Paralympians through the ages, Bridie was annoyed but understood why Mary Ellen Synon, a popular journalist at the *Sunday Independent*, was perceived as writing disparagingly about Sydney 2000. Mary Ellen seemed to imply that disabled athletes were 'grotesque, perverse' and went on to say, 'Surely, physical competition is about finding the best – the fastest, strongest, highest, all that. It is not about finding someone who can wobble their way around a track in a wheelchair or who can swim from one end of a pool to the other by Braille.' Bridie recalls the backlash against Mary Ellen and simply says, 'She didn't understand, maybe she knows now. Mary Ellen Synon's article caused a national reaction, which ironically did us all a massive favour.'

Bridie's friend and Paralympic room-mate Catherine Walsh says of the article, 'It was a badly judged piece of writing, which gained so much traction it funded Athens 2004.'

Bridie bade farewell to her Paralympic career in Sydney. A pre-Games hamstring injury was followed by an unfortunate discus throw, which rebounded off the cage to break her foot.

Catherine Walsh recalls the day. 'The ecstasy of winning my own first medal in Sydney soon turned to agony as Bridie was now in a wheelchair, her golden career now over. That evening, she ate my Pringles, which I had hidden for my post-event celebration. That was understandable. I forgive and try to forget.'

A fortnight after competing in our 2001 Mayfest, tragedy visited Bridie and her family. 'My 37-year-old sister Margaret was walking downtown with her three children when a lorry came down the wrong side of the road. She saw it, and she pushed the children back, but she was killed.'

Bridie stepped in to support her brother-in-law, 'to try and give the children some normality for a few years'.

Her carer role was then interrupted by a serious illness, which left her laid up in Letterkenny General Hospital for three months. Bridie was diagnosed with Crohn's. In 2007, after having part of her bowel removed, Bridie's sister Rosemary nursed her back to health and assisted Bridie with dressings and general care. Tragically, 'Rosemary then mentioned back pain to me and later had some tests. She died within the week. She was forty-seven.'

Throughout it all, Bridie found sport a helpful coping mechanism. From athlete to coach, she began supporting women on the move in sport and worked with the Letterkenny Profiles gym.

Four b/vi athletes have won Paralympic gold for Ireland to date, and all have Donegal connections. Carol Carr's dad, Barney, is from Fanad, while Katie-George Dunlevy's dad, John, is from Glenties. Jason Smyth's grandad, William Hastings, hails from St Johnston, while Bridie is multi-generations Donegal, born, bred and living in St Johnston.

In 2013 Bridie Lynch became the first athlete to be inducted into the Paralympics Ireland Hall of Fame. In 2021 Bridie was inducted into the Vision Sports Ireland Hall of Fame.

25. **Here comes the knight**

Braille chess with Philip Doyle (Mayo).

Sex-toy-cheating stories vibrated through the world of chess in the autumn of 2022. (If you missed how elite chess nuts allegedly cheat, don't worry. *Chess: the Musical, Part Two* is sure to be on a stage near you soon.)

Chess is the centuries-old noble game of kings and queens, where 99.99 per cent of players nowadays are ordinary people who play to win, but not at all costs. If you're looking for the perfect model, the genuine article, Braille chess is your answer.

B/vi players may thank Francis H. Merrick, a wood craftsman and founder of the first Braille chess club in 1902, for creating the modified board. Players could examine the pieces on the board by touch. The black squares are raised slightly above the level of the white squares with a hole drilled in the centre of each square. Each chess piece has a peg in its base, which fits into the holes in the board. The black pieces are distinguished by a small pin on the top. When Braille chess players compete against each other, they share the board. Otherwise, each player uses a separate board and, after making a move, announces it to their opponent. The adapted board remains in widespread use to this day.

The Worcester College 1869 prospectus includes chess in its extracurricular activities for b/vi pupils. However, widespread b/vi chess began with correspondence games at the turn of the twentieth century. Same-day or next-day free delivery of Braille post facilitated correspondence chess across these islands.

Legendary five-times Braille chess Olympian Philip Doyle, a Westport man born with retinitis pigmentosa (RP), is an expert on the game's history in Ireland.

Philip explains: 'In the early years here, there was no organised method of teaching the game. The first players of note – Joe Barret and Joe Byrne – learned chess from Kevin Turner at St Joseph's in Drumcondra in 1914. The next important player at St Joseph's was Willie Breen, who was taught by John Nolan circa 1930.

'I played with and against Willie Breen. He was a very determined, adamant kind of fellow who expected respect. With Joe Barret, he played open competitive chess with North City Chess Club at Dublin's Mountjoy Square in the mid-30s. He was an active member of the Braille Chess Association from its inception in the UK in 1932, where he won several correspondence tournaments. He led the Irish team to our first Braille Chess Olympiad in East Germany in 1964 and represented his country in three subsequent Olympiads. In 1997 we joined Willie for his eightieth-birthday celebrations at Dublin's Ierne Club with the wider chess and b/vi community. Willie remained an active chess player until close to passing away in 2001.'

Meanwhile, 'the Boss' hit town at St Joseph's in 1956. The Boss – not Bruce Springsteen – was Brother Louis Summerling, and he brought in Braille chess boards and tried to teach the game. It was a novelty for the boys, who soon got bored.

Four years later, the Boss returned to chess, this time with major success.

'He was an excellent coach and organiser for young people,' recalls Philip. 'He made it compulsory, which didn't go down well with some of the boys, but I was interested and enjoyed the two classes each week as well as the various tournaments.

'The Boss entered teams into the Leinster Schools Chess Championships. These teams had remarkable success. In 1964 St Joseph's won the Leinster Schools junior title. The following year, they won the senior title. The champions included Eamonn Casey, Des Kenny (later NCBI boss), Sam Wilson, Tim Rea, Martin McGrath and Eugene O'Connor, with some assistance from Tom Dooley. I won the Junior Individual in 1966.'

Braille chess, just like the mainstream game, was dominated for many years by the USSR, eastern Europe and the USA. However, Ireland has a proud record at the Braille Olympiad over eleven tournaments. Philip singles out Weymouth 1968. 'This, I feel, was Ireland's best performance in the Olympiads, with the team playing consistently throughout. The highlights included a draw with the Americans in round two and a whitewash of the Israelis in the final round.'

In major championships, such as the Olympiad, chess combines the eyesight classes of B1, B2 and B3 players.

Ireland's next Olympiad in Yugoslavia almost failed to take off as there were no pennies in the bank. Hans Cohn MBE, a b/vi cross-country skier and Braille chess leader, contacted Jim Walsh, the well-known *Irish Times* b/vi journalist. Jim gave the story legs, which landed our chess players on prime-time TV with Gay Byrne on the longest-running chat show in Europe, *The Late Late Show*. Players Michael Keane and Sean Loftus displayed lightning chess skills before telling their story to Gay. Soon, travel agent Alan Perkins offered to pay for the flights while Tayto donated £200 of crispy notes (circa a crunchy €3,000 today).

Now set up for the 70s and beyond, Braille chess began attracting future senior stars, including Philip.

Philip and I were inseparable once he became my civil service colleague on a snowy November morning in 1977. He's a lifelong lover of GAA and was a one-year-old when his native Mayo last won an All-Ireland in 1951.

He represented Ireland in five Braille chess Olympiads from 1980 to 2004, competing in forty-seven games.

Fundraising was always difficult for the small team of Ireland players. But they had friends in high places. They even made it into the pages of John Glatt's best-selling book *The Chieftains: The Authorised Biography*.

On 12 February 1984 the Chieftains celebrated their twenty-first birthday with a sell-out champagne show at Dublin's National Concert Hall. A slice of programme advertising revenue from the event went to Ireland's Braille Chess Olympiad team. Between the jigs and the reels, Philip Doyle's team received a tidy sum.

At the anniversary, the concert chief of the Chieftains, the late Paddy Maloney, blew out the birthday candles on his uilleann pipes. Four decades on, the flames are now flickering out on organised Braille chess in Ireland. Most of the heroes of yesteryear are now either drawing pensions or happily playing the game in chess heaven.

Philip says, 'Braille chess could re-emerge as our population diversifies and there's a greater east European presence. It's an ideal game for b/vi people.'

In concluding, Philip asked for special 'checkmates' for so many Braille Chess Association (founded 1985) colleagues not already mentioned, including Ernie McElroy, Michael Delaney and Joe McAloon. Also, special acknowledgements to two former association secretaries, Larry Currid and Tim Conlon.

26. You've got a friend in me

Tony Guest (Louth) and John Newman (Longford), featuring road running.

Tony Guest has the distinction of being the first recipient of Hall of Fame awards from both Vision Sports Ireland and Paralympics Ireland. He's our forever friend who was our manager, mentor, guide runner and coach.

Tony is so integrated with the b/vi community that an employee at Irish Blindcraft once asked me if Tony Guest worked as a blind telephonist or one of those new blind physios. Neither is true. Now retired, Tony was a sunroom and conservatory constructor who had no vision impairment.

So, how did an athletics coach at Blackrock AC in Co. Louth end up managing b/vi international teams and becoming president of Paralympics Ireland?

Tony takes up the story, 'A little over forty years ago, I got a phone call from a fella who says, "I hear you do a bit of running. I'm blind and looking for a guide." I was hesitant, but my wife, Anne, who was standing beside me, said, "Why the bloody hell won't you? You're out there helping those who don't need help. He needs help, get out there and guide him."

The caller was John Newman, an absolute gent who persuaded me a few months earlier to guide him in a 10-mile race. I did and will never, ever guide again. It was scary.'

Tony Guest and John Newman became inseparable. In the few short years that followed, they ran the Dublin and London marathons, plus many more major races together. John became close friends with the entire Guest family.

John was also a key member of Tony's athletics club, Blackrock AC, and he produced their regular newsletters. John said of their coastal base, 'Blackrock was a lovely place if only the tide came in.'

As Tony Guest and I recently sipped coffee in a Dublin café, we recounted many John Newman stories. I recalled being awoken at midnight at St Joseph's by the ringing of the school bell. It was John raising the alarm as he had got himself locked into a classroom after late study. Tony remembers John and his teenage tales of hopping over the school wall for a quick pint in the local Cat & Cage pub in Drumcondra.

I reminded Tony of the story about John and the state-of-the-art TV. Tony laughs. 'We were out for a run one Sunday morning and passing through the border market town at Jonesborough in Co. Armagh. John asked if we could return and pick up a TV after our run. When I got home after picking up the television, Anne asked if John had bought a black-and-white or a colour television. Colour, I said. "What does he need a colour TV for? Sure, he can't see it," she said. With that, Anne rang him to find out. John explained that if he "pulled a bird, there's no point at her looking at a cheap black-and-white TV".'

It's no surprise then that the title for this chapter originated from Randy Newman.

On Friday, 31 May 1985, John Newman had lunch with triple Paralympian Pat Kelly in Dundalk. The next day, he headed home to his mother in Granard, Co. Longford, to enjoy the sunny June

Bank Holiday weekend. Overnight, aged just thirty-eight, John Newman passed away after a massive heart attack.

To this day, we, his friends, shudder in shock as we recall our glory days with John. At the time, we founded and funded the John Newman Memorial Trophy, which was awarded annually at Mayfest to our Sports Personality of the Year.

In the year or so before his death, John had introduced Tony to the wider b/vi training group based in the Dublin area. For the next fifteen years, Tony led and coached more than a hundred b/vi people at all levels. Tony also supported the Irish national team manager, Mick McKeon, from 1985 to 1992 before taking over the role himself.

Mick and Tony were a class act. Speaking to me by phone, Mick recalls travelling from his Wexford base for the first time to attend the Saturday athletics sessions. Mick says, 'They were a lovely bunch of people, the athletes and the administrators. There were many good athletes there. I know some thought that because the athletes had guides, they had an advantage while running. They didn't have any advantage and were very skilled athletes. I thoroughly enjoyed coaching with Tony, great memories.'

From 1985 to 2000 – from Rome to Sydney – Tony Guest was a manager of b/vi international teams.

Tony says Seoul was an eye-opener, with the 100m taking over two hours to complete, while Barcelona was big, with a big number of athletes, a big attendance, and a big Irish team with judo in there.

The opening night at Atlanta '96 intrigued Tony. 'A year beforehand, Anne and I holidayed in Toronto and drove from there to Florida via Atlanta, as I wanted to see the Olympic stadium. There was no stadium, just foundations. The night of the Paralympics Opening Ceremony, the stadium looked fantastic. However, we were in the adjoining warm-up area, and I noticed a man in a tractor circling the track. I discovered he was painting the ground green to make it look like grass.'

Sydney was the game-changer for administration. Tony continues: 'We had formed into one unit under the new Irish Paralympic Council, with significant support from the also new Irish Sports Council. We were scientific and professional in our approach. A wonderful games.'

Tony credits the late Anne Ebbs, who unselfishly devoted her entire adult life to growing IWA Sport and the Paralympic movement in Ireland. Tony says of her, 'Anne was the most honest, generous, warm person you could meet. Always with her finger on the button. She built up a wonderful relationship with John Treacy, the head of sport here for twenty-two years. Anne was key to building what is now Paralympics Ireland.'

Des Kenny, champion of all b/vi activity for seven decades, has similar sentiments and adds: 'I saw the IWA and the Paralympic movement as pivotal to how Irish Blind Sports developed.'

Denis Toomey, Vice President, Paralympics Ireland, says of Ann, 'An amazing woman who opened doors for people with disabilities. She never took no for an answer. Through her, I keep fighting and won't accept a no. Ann took the Paralympics from nothing to where it is now.'

After Sydney, Tony Guest was appointed president of the Irish Paralympics Council. Ever humble, Tony says, 'It was an honour for Irish Blind Sports, for the work you all put in over so many years.' Ann Lyster had preceded Tony as chair of the Council. Tony remained president for nine years.

Looking back over five decades with b/vi and disabled athletes in general, Tony concludes, 'It was the best thing that I have ever done. I enjoyed every minute and made lifelong friends. I respected everyone, and I think everyone respected me.'

27. **Off the wall**

What goes on outside the village.

What happens in the village stays in the village, but what about what goes on outside the village?

Gus Dorrington recalls Seoul '88: 'We had finished our events and were hanging out in the "dry" Paralympic Village. Our manager, Mick McKeon, took decisive action and sneaked us through security and into a nearby shanty town. We encountered a guy with a large oil tanker. Mick guessed what was really in the tanker and struck up a deal for crates of Heineken at half a dollar a can. Our new friend not only supplied the beer but gave us a plank to sit on and empty barrels for tables. We were so happy in our private Seoul shebeen. The next night, we returned to our new private pub to find it was overcrowded. Our plank and barrels were now occupied by dozens of Americans. Quickly, our new Seoul mate moved the Americans to a new location and sat us in his private members' lounge. He believed we had brought along the large crowd and gave us a drink on the house.'

Tony Guest recalls the boys 'Seoul searching' for exclusive watches. 'Some picked up "Rolexes" and thought they were the bee's knees. As soon as they got on the plane home, the watches stopped.' Timeless memories!

Mick McKeon recalls Gothenburg '86: 'They had this idea to present medals in this large hall with no atmosphere and no entertainment beforehand. So Ronan Tynan and I got up to sing, and soon we were joined by many more. The organisers weren't happy and made us leave the stage.' Mick's side-kick Tony Guest recently pondered, 'Imagine asking Ronan Tynan, the world-famous tenor, to leave the stage now.'

Mick McKeon recalls the Euros in '85 and travelling to Castel Gandolfo to meet Pope John Paul I. 'Superfan Harry Gorman, who officiated at many Mayfests, was in Rome at another event but decided to join us. A papal official told us not to approach the Pope as he was frail. The Pope comes out and has barely reached the lectern when Harry is up beside him. The security rushed forward, but the Pope said, "It's okay, he's Irish!"'

Martin Kelly can walk right back to Arnhem in 1980 and a chance backstage meeting with the late musician Phil Everly. The late Phil Donnelly, well-known as the Clontarf Cowboy, was on stage with Everly and spotted the Irish tracksuits in the Dutch audience. He called them out and invited them backstage, and now all Martin can do is dream, dream, dream.

It was what's another year for Catherine Walsh, as she recalled Johnny Logan performing at the opening of the 1994 IPC World Championships. While Bonnie Tyler also performed, it was the total eclipse of the 10m diving board which Catherine will never forget. 'Post competition, I headed over to the diving board with teammates Mick Delaney and Trevor O'Connell. We skipped the 2m board and headed straight up for the 10m. Before we dive, Trevor says to wait for him at the bottom as he can't swim. We all plunged, rescued Trevor, and took him to the baby pool.'

Delaney and O'Connell feature in Rahim Nazarali's off-track magic moment, too. 'In Atlanta '96, the escalator in the main tube station was five times bigger than what you'd see in Ireland. Mick Delaney, Trevor O'Connell, and I challenged each other to a race up the down escalator. The escalator won. I also remember persuading a volunteer village buggy driver to allow me to drive his vehicle, me with feck-all sight. I pressed hard on the accelerator and cleared the road in seconds. How nobody was hurt still astonishes me.'

When you sing Ireland's best-known famine song to America's leading organisation for Irish immigrants, you gotta be good. Pat Kelly, unprompted and unrehearsed, was note-perfect when he belted out 'The Fields of Athenry' at the Ancient Order of Hibernians (AOH) post-Paralympic fundraising event on Long Island in 1984. Pat received a standing ovation. Thanks to our early-days member Timmy Rea, who secured the AOH contact for us, the Order raised $35,000 for the b/vi Paralympic team of '84, equivalent to €100,000 today – going for a song.

Another song, where the late Shane McGowan sings 'The boys of the NYPD choir were singing "Galway Bay"' is indeed a fairy tale. As most people now realise, there was no NYPD choir, but I can assure you there is an NYPD Emerald Society Pipe and Drums Band, a few of whose members feature in the 'Fairytale of New York' video. I met these guys, and we shared a night on the town like no other.

A few of us were giddy at a post-Paralympics posh 'do' in central Manhattan. Exiting the restrooms, we bumped into the off-duty Emerald boys, who invited us into the car lot, where they had a booty of booze. Soon, those of us who could see a little saw double lines, but we still parked ourselves there for the night. Later, led by our hosts, we embarked on a mighty pub crawl, which lasted until dawn. Oh, what a night, late June 1984.

28. Wheelin' in the years

Tandem cycling.

Award-winning volunteer Benny Grogan was fifty-one before he met a blind person for the first time.

'I fundraised and travelled to Florida with Vision Ireland's Blazing Saddles team in 1993. The tandem pilot for Kerry's Toddy Carey had dropped out, so they needed a substitute. I volunteered, although I never piloted a tandem and never met a blind person ever.'

Benny is a lifelong lover of sport who, in 1966, won a Leinster GAA Junior Football County Championship title with Louth. Two years later, he captained St Kevin's GAA Club, Philipstown, Co. Louth, to a county title. In February 2019 Benny was inducted into the Vision Sports Ireland Hall of Fame.

In the 1970s Benny and his friend, the late Kevin Boylan, driven by the needs of a local family, organised a 75-km local cycle for Cystic Fibrosis Ireland. They continued the cycle annually into the 80s, raising more than £40,000 (equivalent to €350,000 today).

From 1993 onwards, Benny travelled the world – Canada, Thailand, Malaysia, South Africa, Europe and the USA – piloting b/vi cyclists for Vision Ireland's Blazing Saddles. In 1997 he introduced Marion Finegan to tandem cycling. Marion became his new tandem partner, indeed his partner for life.

Marion was Secretary of the Louth Branch of Vision Ireland for sixteen years. As legendary para-athlete Pat Kelly explains, 'Marion was extraordinary. She was everything to everybody in the north-east, organising parties, outings and constantly taking care of the welfare of b/vi people. She was always there for you, no matter what time of day.'

Marion says, 'In the early 90s, my life took a turn as I was losing sight due to diabetes. I gravitated towards Vision Ireland and loved being Louth secretary.

'Benny persuaded me to cycle in the 1997 Blazing Saddles Rockies trip from Calgary to Vancouver. My brother lives in British Columbia, so it was attractive. I had no cycling background and began training with Benny.'

After the Rockies, Marion joined Benny as the Saddles blazed the world.

The larger-than-life Eamon Duffy founded Blazing Saddles in 1989. Over two decades, they cycled in over forty countries, grossing millions for Vision Ireland. Tony Lynch, a veteran Vision Ireland volunteer in the north-east, says, 'Eamon Duffy created massive awareness of blindness in Ireland and put b/vi tandem cycling on the map.'

Eamon told me recently, 'While our goal was to support Vision Ireland and part-fund their training centre, the key for me was getting blind and partially-sighted people on tandems.

'Over twenty years, five TV documentaries were aired on Blazing Saddles. Also, we featured on many RTÉ Radio programmes, including shows with Gay Byrne, Joe Duffy, Pat Kenny and Ian Dempsey. I must credit RTÉ head Liam Millar for his support.

'My takeaway from those two magnificent decades: friendships. I met so many blind and visually impaired people, and we are lifelong friends. What more could you ask for in life?'

Pat Kelly recalls a Saddles colleague being arrested in California for a traffic offence and being brought into the precinct for questioning. 'Then a cop comes out and asks if our colleague was with that fella Eamon Duffy. Yes! He was immediately released and told never to U-turn on a freeway again.'

Blazing Saddles left many legacies, including Louth WATCH (Walking and Tandem Cycling for Health), founded by Danny McSherry over a decade ago.

Pat Kelly says, 'Danny was our go-to leading volunteer and key organiser who started the Newry and Mourne WATCH Club. Through his work with RNIB, he was aware of European cross-border funding. Danny set us up and arranged finance. He appointed Benny as our chairperson. Each year, as the springtime clock goes forward, we head off on local Saturday cycles. We also cycle the country for charity as a group and individually.'

Danny McSherry appointed Maureen Madden as Louth WATCH Secretary and, with his friend Michael McAteer, piloted her on her first Mizen to Malin Cycle.

Maureen Madden recalls, 'That was a fantastic cycle. I had tandem-cycled to raise funds for our school tour at Merrion when I was sixteen. That was it for twenty-five years until I joined up with the last Blazing Saddles trip to Majorca. I now cycle and walk to take care of my well-being. It keeps me healthy.'

Maureen is the volunteer secretary every committee would welcome with open arms.

In a 2023 survey conducted by DCU in association with Vision Ireland and Vision Sports Ireland, an impressive 9.4 per cent of 345 respondents – almost one in ten – chose tandem cycling as a favourite activity.

Tandem cycling is an ideal activity that can be shared with family and friends. The pilot complements the stoker and vice-versa. It is not inexpensive. The average cost of a sturdy new tandem is €3,000, or rock bottom, €500 second-hand. Our elite cyclists could pay more than €20,000 for a customised racer.

If you're interested, your best bet is to get a short-term tandem loan. Vision Sports Ireland and the small tandem community will sort it out for you. If you get hooked and have a few bob you could purchase, but it is always best to seek advice to ensure you get the value and it.

In the era of smart technology and wearables, voice-activated equipment is available to measure speed, wattage, distance and much more.

Tandem cycling on open, busy roads can be tricky. 'Safety first,' says Tony Lynch, the Louth WATCH chairperson and leading Vision Ireland fundraiser. 'As a pilot, you're responsible for the person on the back. Tandems can reach serious speeds of 55km per hour and even more. But safety trumps speed every time.'

Stoker Marion Finegan agrees. 'But I've never been scared with Benny Grogan. I have full confidence and know he'll tell me of bumps, twists and turns. Tandems need space. We all wear hi-vis with *tandem cyclist* inscriptions.'

Pat Kelly concludes, 'Pilots mean everything to us. The more pilots we have, the more b/vi people could cycle. It's a great healthy social activity where you can see the country, maybe the world.'

Aside from Louth WATCH, tandem groups have popped up in Ireland in Galway, Dublin and Belfast. Many b/vi tandem cyclists join local cycling clubs and weekend groups.

Road- and pursuit-tandem cycling is a Paralympic sport. While stokers are classified as B1, B2 and B3, these classes are merged and compete as one.

29. Don't stop believin'

Rahim Nazarali (Dublin/Kenya), featuring judo.

You'll never stop believing once you meet Rahim Nazarali, the model ambassador for b/vi sport.

He has played it all, administered it all, coached some and influenced many. While now at ease in the gym or going for a swim, he was instrumental in promoting adapted sport here, especially judo and water sports.

Rahim was born in 1978 in Nairobi, Kenya. His mum is from Glasnevin in Dublin, while his late dad is of Indian descent.

'It took a while for my parents to realise I had a vision impairment. I was born two months premature. They gave me too much oxygen to keep me alive, and that affected my vision.

'The family doctor was in my grandparents' restaurant one day, and he commented that I wasn't responding to stimuli properly. My parents acted quickly, had me tested in Kenya and then flew me to London for assessment. My diagnosis was retrolental fibroplasia with resultant glaucoma with a probability of further vision loss through life.'

Rahim was eight months old when his parents chose Ireland as the best location to raise him. By age four, he was enrolled as a day pupil at St Mary's, Merrion; at age seven, he was at St Joseph's in Drumcondra. He loved the sports facilities in both schools, where he enjoyed swimming, running and football.

At age twelve, Rahim's family emigrated to Canada. 'Many of our relations had moved from Kenya to Canada and were keen that we join them. Years earlier, dictator Idi Amin had kicked many Asians out of Uganda, and this spooked Kenyan Asian people. We never got to settle as my dad couldn't sell his Dublin business, so we returned to Ireland after six months.'

Rahim was greatly influenced by his short time in mainstream schooling in Edmonton, Alberta, Canada. He says, 'It was an amazing experience. They had lots of funding to include pupils with disabilities. They placed a big emphasis on me being involved in sport. Hockey was interesting. They had a guide beside me to ensure I was in the game against fully-sighted classmates. For baseball, we used an adapted larger ball, which made it easier for me. It was my first taste of inclusion. I wasn't happy to return to Ireland as mainstreaming and inclusion were only in their infancy here in the early 90s.'

Rahim returned to the Drumcondra campus and attended the post-primary Rosmini Community School, which promoted GAA and basketball. 'As these sports didn't suit me, Jack Bracken, a sports-mad resource worker, and Norman Caprani, a judo coach, coaxed me into competitive judo.

'Soon I was in the gym four days a week, running most days and playing judo. Norman ran with me most days. Jack, meanwhile, arranged funding through Vision Sports Ireland for me to travel to weekend mainstream judo competitions.'

There are minimal rule adaptations governing b/vi judokas. Standard body weight categories apply. In mainstream judo, when the referee gives the 'Hajime' command, play begins.

However, where b/vi judokas are involved, the referee gives the Hajime instruction twice. The first time is to alert the b/vi player to locate the opponent's suit grips, and the second time to let the match begin. For para-judo eyesight classification, Judokas who have a visual acuity of less than or equal to LogMAR 2.6 in binocular vision compete in the J1 class, while athletes who have a visual acuity within the range between LogMAR 1.3 and 2.5 with binocular vision, or with a binocular visual field of 60 degrees or less in diameter compete against each other in the J2 class.

In 1995 Rahim competed in a Paralympic qualifier in Spain and won bronze in his weight category. The following year, he was on the plane for Atlanta '96.

'Atlanta? It was an amazing experience,' he recalls. 'I was the youngest on the team at eighteen. While I prepared well, I don't think I realised how significant the event was. Looking back now, I realise what an achievement it was to be there, to be a Paralympian.'

Rahim was a finalist in the 78kg class and won his last sixteen contests, but he was defeated at the quarter-final stage. A year later, he also reached the last eight in the IBSA European Championships.

In May 1999 Rahim won three of his fights at the Sydney 2000 qualifiers in Austria. He understood he had qualified for Sydney. Later that year, IBSA held a new qualifying competition. Rahim bowed out in controversy. The officials had instructed him to wear the wrong colour judo suit. A hasty change of wardrobe was too late for Rahim, as he became distracted and lost his final qualifying bout.

Irish judokas competed at four Paralympic Games from 1992 to 2004. Tony White, from Malahide in Dublin, was capped three times. Tim Culhane, from neighbouring Portmarnock, was twice a

Paralympian and won silver at the 1999 European Championships in Austria.

Following a series of serious injuries, Rahim stepped back from judo in 2003, only to return ten years later to train with and coach a new team of Irish b/vi judo players.

Off the mat, Rahim loves downhill skiing, water-skiing and surfing. He competed in the 2010 Limerick City Marathon. Rahim also loves long walks alongside canals. In 2013 he walked along the entire Royal Canal. In 2014 he also completed a walk along the Grand Canal. Ten years later, he repeated his Royal journey with friends Robert Burke and Dawn Murtagh. Their first stop was in Maynooth, where we had a lovely home BBQ in my back garden. Rahim has also dabbled in tandems and b/vi tennis.

In the boardroom, Rahim has been a member of the Irish Paralympic Council and Vision Sports Ireland. For fourteen years, he was Adult and Child Liaison Officer at Vision Sports Ireland, where he also worked for a short time as Sports Development Officer.

Rahim is engaged to top multi-sport athlete Tina Paulick.

For Rahim, sport has been the gateway to integration and inclusion. 'I was a boarder with few friends beyond the school walls. School in Canada was my springboard, but the big game-changer was when I joined Portmarnock Judo Club and got to train, compete and socialise with some truly great people.

'I live and love sport. If you haven't found the great indoors and outdoors, try it out. Try everything, and you're sure to find something that works. It will be your passport to making new friends and living a full life,' Rahim concludes.

30. **Against all odds**

Hosting 1993 European Athletics Championships, Dublin, with Mick McKeon (Wexford), Ann Lyster (Monaghan) and Tony Lyster (Dublin).

They said it couldn't be done. They were wrong.

That five-year-old Vision Sports Ireland, a tiny not-for-profit, volunteer-led organisation, could host the biggest event for b/vi sportspeople in the world in 1993 was incredible.

On 7 September 1993, An Taoiseach, the late Albert Reynolds, officially opened the IBSA European Athletics Championships, and 1,500 people turned up to witness history.

Three hundred athletes from twenty-one nations marched in the opening ceremony on a very wet afternoon. The week-long event was a runaway success.

I recently caught up with event director Ann Lyster and her husband, Tony, the event PRO. They spoke in unison when they told me, 'It should have failed.' Ann continues: 'Everything was against us. Amid it all, we had the sad passing of Liam Clifford, who was our "Mr Belfield". Liam had taken care of all our needs there for many years, a venue where we regularly trained and competed.

'After Liam, Belfield facilities fell into chaos, and we had to re-negotiate everything. They weren't used to hosting international championships in those days. There were no flag poles, no flags, no suitable admin area, no press area and no sheltered viewing stand. The list was endless. Away from Belfield, eastern Europe had a new landscape with resulting new flags, anthems, and visa requirements.'

Tony and Ann Lyster met while Ann was a pupil at Merrion (Ann's eye condition is albinism). Tony recalls, 'Had the Pope not come to Ireland in '79, I wouldn't have met Ann. I joined the Colleges Volunteer Corps as a steward for the visit. When the Pope went home, I continued with the "Corps" and joined them in visiting St Mary's in Merrion on a regular basis.'

'My first impression,' recalled Ann, 'I explained to my friend Mags Hughes, who had no sight, that Tony was a scrawny one in a red jumper.'

Five years later, Tony and Ann married.

Ann's interest in athletics and Tony's in cycling soon saw them engage with b/vi sport. From 1988 to 2004 and from 2010 to 2015, Tony and Ann Lyster have performed every executive role possible at Vision Sports Ireland. Ann was also chairperson of the Irish Paralympic Council. They gave half their extended Donabate, Dublin home to office and storage for b/vi sport.

At the 1993 Europeans, Tony's skills as a graphic designer came into play as he designed the official logo, medals, programme and much more.

Following the official opening of the 1993 championships, as event secretary, I escorted the Taoiseach to his car. Just then, a senior Irish official informed me that the first field event, the long jump, had been cancelled as it was not up to IBSA standards.

Our senior official had a plan. Firstly, he collared another Joe, Joe Walsh, dad of Catherine Walsh, our star Paralympian. Joe knew exactly who could speedily construct a championship-standard long jump area.

Next, our senior official convened a technical meeting, which I facilitated. To show some hospitality, we brought in ample vodka. To nobody's surprise it was a long meeting, which ended in the darkest hours with a visit to Joe Walsh's construction site. The IBSA official signed off on the long jump, no doubt a staggering decision!

After skipping over the long-jump challenge, Joe Walsh was determined to overcome the marathon wall. How could a 42km race be run down the busy N11 motorway from Belfield to Bray and back?

Catherine Walsh recalls: 'My dad wasn't the better of that. He was worried about the serious risks and used his wide network to bring in as many stewards as possible. He would have preferred if it was run through a closed-gate Phoenix Park.'

At dawn on Saturday, 11 September 1993, the race was run successfully with Joe's leadership, his army, *An Garda Síochána* and RTÉ Radio One and Two, who barraged motorists with information.

Event funding was extraordinarily successful, with support from dozens of sources, including the Irish government, Apple, Vision Ireland, the Variety Club of Ireland and the EU.

Oh yes, the EU. They gave us ten grand and a balloon.

Tony Lyster remembers: 'We gathered a team of b/vi volunteers to anchor the EU hot air balloon. All was fine until a gust of wind caused the balloon to lift from the ground. We could have lost half of our team that day, the world's first blind astronauts in space.'

While researching this book, I was knocked out by the number of people who, unprompted, singled out these championships. Many said it was a life highlight.

Bringing the Euros to Dublin was a dream come true for me. Since my silver success in Varna '83, I was convinced Ireland could host these championships. Many others who believed came on board, including future president of Bord Lúthchleas na hÉireann (BLE) – the predecessor of Athletics Ireland – Mick McKeon.

I found Mick through Brendan Foreman, the legendary BLE. and Olympic Council of Ireland official. From the off, Mick was fired up to host the Europeans.

'The huge success of Vision Sports Ireland was the Europeans,' Mick McKeon recalled on the 30th anniversary of the Games. 'I still hear from people, athletes and officials from near and far who enjoyed these Games so much. We had a great organising team, who were probably under-appreciated. The whole thing was done right and yet done in a typical relaxed, friendly, Irish way.

'Like all major complex events, it was only weeks later, years later, that we began to realise and appreciate what we had achieved. It was just fantastic.'

A total of 5,000 spectators attended the visit of our championship's patron, President Mary Robinson. Mrs Robinson saw a world record being broken. She was truly overwhelmed.

President Robinson subsequently became the Honorary Patron of Vision Sports Ireland.

Immediately after the Games, our own president, Liam Nolan, was elected Secretary of IBSA Europe and later hosted a major IBSA meeting in Dublin.

I have one lovely personal moment from those Europeans.

As the presidential visit ended, I was at the back of the massive crowd. I witnessed Mary Robinson head for the state car, accompanied by her mentor, the late Bride Rosney, educator and principal at my Rosmini school, for several years. The president was thirty minutes behind schedule, and Bride had a packed diary. Next, the president made a U-turn. Led by our president, Liam Nolan, she headed straight through the crowd towards where I was with my wife, Grainne, holding our two babies, Claire and Christopher. Liam said, 'President Robinson, you must meet Joe Geraghty.'

Gosh, I was so embarrassed but amazed by her warmth and interest. She personally thanked me for the brief that I provided to her office. Liam Nolan later told me that it made his day to spot me. It made my day, too.

31. Two outta three ain't bad

Catherine Walsh (Dublin), including para-athletics, para-triathlon and tandem cycling.

'I'd like to think I could beat anybody at anything on any day,' laughs record-breaking seven-time Paralympian Catherine Walsh. We are sipping coffee in a café bar in her hometown of Swords, Co. Dublin.

Make no mistake. Catherine is one of the warmest people you'll meet. But, when she competes, she holds the iron fist in the velvet glove. She'll outbox you, outfox you, jump higher, further and be first over the line in the velodrome, on the athletics track or on the road at the Dublin Marathon.

She is the first Irish woman to compete at seven Paralympic Games.

Summing up three decades of international competition, Catherine says, 'I won medals in athletics and cycling and became Ireland's first para-triathlete. Thinking of the medals, I suppose two out of three sports ain't bad.'

Catherine, daughter of our renowned volunteers Joe and Bernie Walsh, was born with albinism and is the second-youngest of eight siblings, 'I was born into an athletics club. My mum and dad were always participating and organising. During my childhood, we had to replace the floor in our kitchen twice because of our family skipping competitions.'

Catherine attended mainstream schooling before enrolling at St Mary's in Merrion at age ten. Two years later, she began her competitive career with race walking at the community games.

At age sixteen she was selected to represent Ireland at the 1990 IPC World Championships in the Netherlands.

1990 was a crazy year for Catherine. Following her successful debut at the World Games, she also began training as a chartered physiotherapist in London. 'Leaving home was difficult, but British Paralympian Sharon Bolton took me under her wing and set me up for all my sports and leisure needs.'

Catherine was soon jetting to Paralympic Games and world and regional championships, including France ('91, '02 and '07), Spain ('92, '95 and '98), Germany ('94), USA ('96, '12 and '15), Italy ('97), Portugal ('99), Australia ('00), Poland ('01), Greece ('04), Finland ('05), China ('08), the UK ('09 and '12) and Brazil ('16).

She explains: 'At the IPC Worlds in Madrid in '98, I didn't medal. However, a Canadian girl on the podium with my teammate Bridie Lynch for the pentathlon suggested, "the three of us must be on the podium together in Sydney 2000". If the Canadian girl believed in me, so must I.

'Sydney was an adventure. By then, there were more countries, more competitors, and fewer places available to the Irish team. For me, it was go for broke or give it up. I put everything aside for Sydney and engaged in nutrition, physiological and general sports science like never before.

'The Australians really got behind Sydney with a full stadium each night. I was down for athletics and the pentathlon. My first four events, the 100m, shot-put, long jump and discus, went well, and I lay in fifth position. Going into the final event, the 800m, there was a lot of shenanigans between officials. I ignored it, kept calm, and ran the race of my life. I won and moved up to third overall. Bronze, my first Paralympic medal. I was over the moon.

'Coming home was fantastic. My mum and dad literally met me off the plane. The number of people waiting at the airport was amazing. There wasn't a day during the following six months when somebody didn't come up to me to congratulate me.'

Catherine's last international athletics medal was gold at 800m at the IPC European Championships in Poland in 2001. Three years later, she represented Ireland at the Paralympic Games in Athens and followed up a year later at the IPC Europeans in Finland.

Catherine married Wally in 1999. In 2003 she gave birth to Alison. Three years later, Conor arrived.

With family first, she still missed sport and had a yearning to compete in triathlons. Her friend and Paralympic teammate Michael Delaney lured her into para-cycling, promising her that hotels and facilities were much better than for track and fielders.

'Adjusting to tandem cycling was a real learning challenge. Working in couples with cycling pilots like Joanna Hickey and Caroline Ryan, we had to adjust to each other's schedules and build compatible relationships. The volume of travel was enormous. We had several falls. I once broke my wrist.'

Catherine competed in the 2007 UCI World Para-cycling Championships and the Paralympics in Beijing a year later. She was now in the top ten of world female tandem stokers, and medals were dangling in front of her. Her first cycling medal was silver at the 2009 UCI World Para-cycling Championships in Manchester.

Teaming up with Fran Meehan in 2011 proved to be the golden ticket. Fran was an accomplished athlete who, like Catherine, progressed to cycling. Within twelve months, they had won gold in the individual track pursuit at the UCI World Para-cycling Championships in LA.

'LA was just magic, such buzz, rainbow jersey, gold.'

London 2012? 'Amazing, all my family stayed over. In the track pursuit, we broke the world record but were pipped by the New Zealand team, whom we beat in LA. This was Ireland's first-ever cycling track medal. Later, we won bronze at the road time trials at Brands Hatch. After the Games, we brought the medals back to my small local pub in London. The champagne flowed, and only then did I realise what Fran and I had achieved.'

'After London, I said, "I'm done." I had said that after each Paralympics since Sydney. Then came the lure of the para-triathlon and a return to multi-eventing. If I could run and cycle, I could swim. The truth was swimming was far more technical than I had realised. Thankfully, Frank Cullinan and Eamonn Tilley sorted me.'

'Before we knew it, Eamonn Tilley and Triathlon Ireland (TI) persuaded us to try for Rio. We qualified for the 2015 World Championships in Detroit and eventually qualified for Rio 2016 as Ireland's first-ever Paralympic triathletes. We finished eighth overall.'

For twenty-six years, Catherine Walsh had trailblazed, but finally, those spokes and spikes have been put aside. Never far from Paralympics, she dabbled in TV punditry for Tokyo 2020. For Paris 2024, she is chair of the Paralympics Ireland Athletes Committee. Her focus is on supporting and facilitating Team Ireland athletes to ensure they can deliver at the highest level in France.

Catherine is a medical classifier at Paralympics Ireland. She is also qualified as a Level 1 athletics and triathlon coach and is chair of the triathlon club Fingal Tri.

'If you're not learning or pushing for a challenge, you're standing still. However, you need variety and a work-life balance.

'My family, my coaches, many people have made huge sacrifices to support me and my sporting life. I feel the least I can do is put something back in of what I took out.'

Catherine Walsh is the gift to disability sport who keeps on giving.

32. We are family

With Joe Walsh and Bernie Walsh (Dublin), the Cusack family (Waterford) and Bernie Everard (Kildare).

How relevant are relatives in supporting b/vi sportspeople? Relatively relevant? Totally relevant? Relatives are the first, the last; they're everything.

Joe Walsh loved and played all sports: boxing, GAA, rugby, athletics. With his wife, Bernie, he established an athletics club in their hometown of Swords five decades ago. In addition, they kept everyone on their feet as they established local community games and 'Meet and Train' groups in the area.

Both Joe and Bernie were active in Vision Sports Ireland and officiated at every Mayfest from 1984 to 2013. Their son Tom and daughter Catherine are celebrated sportspeople and active Vision Sports supporters. They were instrumental in organising the 1993 IBSA European Athletics Championships for the Blind in Dublin.

Joe played a major role in the formation of Athletics Ireland, while Bernie managed Ireland teams at international competition level for b/vi athletes, including the 1996 Paralympic Games in Atlanta. Their favourite day of the week was Tuesday, when they coached young b/vi children from St Joseph's at the Morton Stadium, Santry.

Bernie is now enjoying retirement and getting out and about with her friends. Sadly, Joe passed away in 2022.

I first met Ann Cusack and her husband Liam and their wonderful family, owners of the Granville Hotel on Meagher's Quay in Waterford city, a decade ago.

Ann is queen of the family; husband Liam and daughter Fiona are always by her side, while her grandson, Dean, and mum, Jacqui, are the reason they became so active in b/vi sport.

In recent Mayfest years, they have been running the advice and hospitality tent. However, in yesteryear, Ann sat on our Mayfest committee where, amid the serious organisation, we had fun. When we were short of ties for the three-legged race, Ann delivered some old black tights.

Both Ann and Fiona were key members of the Vision Sports Ireland board and played a significant role in b/vi sport modernisation. They guide, advise and are the conscience of our movement.

Bernie Everard, another ex-director, searched Google in 2014 and found Vision Sports Ireland. She wanted to help her brother-in-law Shane, who was losing sight due to a slow-developing brain tumour. Shane was MD of Corporate Sport and Leisure and entertained business clients at all the top sporting events.

'Shane was forty-four when he received the diagnosis,' recalls Bernie. 'I remember the day. We were preparing to have a family celebration in Las Vegas. After being told he had a brain tumour, Shane just said, "So we might have to postpone Las Vegas for a while." He just couldn't understand or retain information.'

Shortly after the diagnosis, Bernie contacted me at Vision Sports, and I offered some advice on cycling and swimming. Shane and I then met up for a pint. Bernie, her sister Trish – Shane's wife – her husband Martin and some friends raised money to purchase a tandem. They raised a massive surplus, which they donated to Vision Sports, now also the home of Shane's tandem.

Three months after attending Mayfest 2015 with his family, Shane passed away.

Bernie designed and donated the Shane Clyne Memorial Trophy to Vision Sports. After presenting the trophy to the top tandem cyclists at Mayfest 2017, she heard the cry of help for funds from Vision Sports Ireland president Prof. Michael O'Keeffe.

'I had a lightbulb moment. I rang you and asked what Vision Sports could do with €60-70k. We set about applying to be the chosen charity for the 2018 Maynooth Students for Charity Galway Cycle. We came second overall but returned the following year to win the nomination.' In June, while Bernie was in Glastonbury enjoying Kylie Minogue, I received a cheque for Vision Sports for €65,000 from the Galway Cycle. I should be so lucky, lucky, lucky, lucky.

Bernie is a big admirer of Jason Smyth as well as Kylie. 'I was a sprinter myself, so, keenly followed Jason. I just couldn't believe he came to Maynooth to lead the pitch for our cycle. Then Katie-George Dunlevy cycled with us to Galway and back. She was so down to earth and warm, chatting with us all.'

Looking towards the future, Bernie says, 'There is a wonderful group of youth coming through Vision Sports. There's a bright future ahead. A new Jason or Katie-George, don't rule it out.

Féach in the Republic and Angel Eyes in the North are parent-led organisations that connect, inform and empower. As a vision-impaired person with vision-impaired children, some of my best chats have been with fellow parents. I highly recommend contacting either or both organisations as they have a wealth of knowledge, experience and supports there for all of us.

I have had the honour and pleasure of knowing so many relatives of b/vi sportspeople throughout the years, and they don't just take care of their family; they support our extended b/vi family to a level way above any of our expectations. Believe me, I'd love to list them here, but I know I'd miss out on some good friends, so that's not going to happen. We have had many hurdles to overcome, yet together, we've shared many dreams that have become reality. We are family.

33. Annie's song

Kathleen Donnelly with daughter Annie Donnelly (Tipperary), including swimming and tandem cycling.

'Finding Vision Sports means I no longer have to sit on the sidelines,' Annie Donnelly told viewers of RTÉ TV's hit show *Operation Transformation* in September 2017.

Annie was then eight years old and was explaining how she watched her school friends play sports, but she didn't know how to participate. As Annie says, 'I didn't know how to fix it. They didn't know how to fix it.'

Then the Vision Sports Ireland cavalry arrived, led by Nick Harrison of the FAI. He unleashed his bag of adaptive sport tricks and balls of all sizes and colours, which bounced all over the hall. Annie never looked back.

Dozens of sporting activities later, I recently took to the sideline and checked in with the teenage Annie and her mum.

Annie is from Horse and Jockey, Co. Tipperary, and is the first daughter of Kathleen and Eamonn Donnelly. Bill is her younger sibling.

'Annie was diagnosed with achromatopsia just after her first birthday,' Kathleen told me. Annie then explains: 'Achromatopsia may contain a few conditions, including nystagmus, a shaking in the eye. There's low visual activity, poor light sensitivity and depth

Tony Guest, President of Paralympics Ireland 2000–10 and manager of Irish blind/vi international teams for two decades is inducted into the Paralympics Ireland Hall of Fame, 2013. Photo: Sportsfile.

Blind/vi judoka Tony White competed in three Paralympic Games. Photo: Vision Ireland Insight.

Record seven-times Paralympian Catherine Walsh jumps to success at the 2005 25th Anniversary Vision Sports Ireland Mayfest. Photo: Vision Ireland Insight.

At Mayfest 2015 at Mount Anville School in Goatstown, the Clyne family from Maynooth donate €3,000 to Vision Sports Ireland. Left to right: Robert Dobbyn, Shane Clyne and Trish Clyne. Photo: Eamonn McGee.

'Finding Vision Sports means I no longer have to sit on the sidelines.' Eight-year-old Annie Donnelly finding football at Mayfest 2017. Photo: Vision Sports Ireland.

President Michael D. Higgins opened Vision Sports Ireland Mayfest 2016. President of Vision Sports Ireland Prof. Michael O'Keeffe is by his side. Photo: Lorraine O'Connor.

In for the kill, in for the thrill. Blind footballers Paul Costello (left) and Donnacha McCarthy (right). Photo: Vision Sports Ireland.

Wally Roode bowls 'em out at Mayfest 2014. Photo: Karl Leonard.

Leading Rally Ireland navigator Sara McFadden moves to the driving seat at Vision Sports Ireland's Zero Limits at Mondello Park 2023. Photo: Vision Sports Ireland.

I only want to tee with you – Rory McIlroy with (left to right) blind golf guide Scott Gardiner, Rory, Michael Gardiner (blind golf player) and Paul O'Rahilly (player). Photo: Paul O'Rahilly.

Babs Weiberg serves at Vi Tennis. Photo: Babs Weiberg.

'Sailing is a pleasure. When you can't drive, it's simply great to get on the water, steer the boat and harness the wind to take you where you want to go.' Hilary Devlin sails away. Photo: Hilary Devlin.

At the Paris World Para-swimming Championships 2023 Róisín Ní Riain from Limerick displays the gold and the silver. She won gold at the S13 100m backstroke and silver at the 100m butterfly. Photo: Sportsfile.

Vision Sports Ireland introduced a government-approved 'pass-sport' during the Covid pandemic to enable b/vi people to play sport with designated guides. Here Sarah and Maya take exercise. Photo: Vision Sports Ireland.

Difficulties in identifying the finish line means b/vi sprinters are reluctant to dip for victory. At Tokyo 2020 Jason Smyth dipped to win his final Paralympic gold. Photo: Sportsfile.

Joe Geraghty and family. Left to right: Chris (son), Katie, Ellie and Claire (daughters), Grainne (wife) and Joe. Photo: Graham Philips.

perception. I'm colourblind. I wear orange glasses to protect my eyes from the light.'

Kathleen adds, 'It's a rare hereditary condition. You could say Eamonn and I had a bad cell each. I passed one down, Eamonn passed one down, and they both met.'

The late Prof. Michael O'Keeffe, who diagnosed the condition, had one piece of advice for Kathleen: 'Mom, don't wrap her up in cotton wool!' When Eamonn asked the legendary professor about exposure to sun on holidays, more sound advice was issued: 'She won't thank you in the future if she's in college and wants to go travelling with her friends and she has no experience of sun holidays.'

Sport for b/vi people can be like a sun holiday. Play by adapted rules, and you can have the time of your life.

Once Annie found Vision Sports, it was onwards and upwards. She explains: 'Nick Harrison invited me to Mayfest 2017, where I tried tandem cycling, swimming, judo, tennis, football and running.'

Annie and Kathleen both say that travelling to Mayfest was the game-changer. 'So many amazing things happened that day,' recalls Annie. 'I ran a lap of the track with Jason Smyth. Also, Danny McSherry, an avid tandem pilot, very generously loaned us a tandem and told us we could have it if we used it. My dad and I use it regularly.'

Annie and Eamonn take part in charity cycles, including Billy Shanahan's annual Trip to Tipp for Vision Ireland, the HMV Cycle for Irish Guide Dogs, and the Maynooth Students for Charity Galway Cycle for Vision Sports Ireland.

Annie was the lucky duckling the day she met Eamonn Tilley and Frank Cullinan: She says, 'At the *Operation Transformation* filming, triathlon coach Eamonn Tilley introduced me to swimming with one-to-one instruction. Later, Frank Cullinan invited me to join his swim group in Dublin. Frank was such a good teacher. I was swimming lengths after a few lessons. I travelled to Dublin each Friday to train with him. I had tried to learn to swim in Tipperary, but I was scared as I couldn't see where my swim teacher was poolside. Thanks to Frank, and Eamonn, I can now swim in Tipperary and join the Vision Sports Portlaoise swim sessions on a regular basis.

'I love any water sports. Through Vision Sports, I have been kayaking, canoeing and stand-up paddleboarding. I also love rock-climbing.'

Travelling cross-country clocked up huge mileage for Annie and her family. Kathleen was circumspect at first but is now delighted with Annie's progress. 'Aside from swimming, we tried athletics and GAA at home, but none worked. Once we got into the loop of Vision Sports, it all worked out. Travel was tough and became a way of life, but it was worth the smile on Annie's face. Back in Tipperary, Annie can now go with her friends to the pool. She is confident in the water.

'For Eamonn and I, it was beneficial to meet other parents and share stories. We learned so much, particularly from former Vision Sports board member Sandra Watts, who was a wealth of support and information. All the parents were so helpful.

'Even though Annie is in mainstream schooling, it is hugely important that she meets other b/vi kids. They're all together and drive each other to excel at whatever they choose.'

One of Annie's school highlights was bringing her classmates to the Vision Sports Inclusion Games at the University of Limerick (UL) sports campus in December 2019.

'My classmates were so excited. I'll never forget the day our teacher came in with the permission slips. She said we were going to UL because of Annie. My friends were so grateful and kept saying "thank you, Annie!"'

With fourteen other Munster mainstream school classes b/vi pupils attended, Annie and her classmates played adapted tennis, football and athletics. They also went swimming and had a fun tug-of-war. The event was sponsored by the late Prof. Michael O'Keeffe and his friends, as well as the Maynooth the Charity for Cycle.

Now attending post-primary school, Annie was the 2022 first-year student of the year. At the end-of-year awards, the school principal explained that while Annie isn't on the school GAA, basketball, rugby, or soccer teams, she is an active sportsperson in her own right and a recent recipient of the Vision Sports Ireland Leadership in Sport award.

Annie says, 'A lot of people at my new school were unaware I was a sportsperson. Now they know.'

Sport has given Annie a passport to meet her heroes, including Jason Smyth, Roy Keane, Katie-George Dunlevy and Róisín Ní Riain.

Looking to the future, Annie says, 'I hope to go to college, go into business, and I'm hoping someday I can work with Vision Ireland and Vision Sports Ireland. Sport gives me freedom, and I can't imagine a life without it.'

As Kathleen puts it, 'Sport is you, Annie.'

34. Our eyes adored you

Prof. Michael O'Keeffe, President, Vision Sports Ireland 2015–23.

'I came across a quote recently about Dad, credited on Vision Sports Ireland's website, when he accepted the role as president of Vision Sports Ireland. The quote was by a colleague of his, and it said. "When God made Prof. O'Keeffe, he must have thrown away the mould because we've never seen anything like him around here ever since."'
The opening words of Isabelle O'Keeffe, daughter of the late Prof. Michael O'Keeffe, in her eulogy at his funeral on 28 January 2023.

Isabelle was quoting from an article I wrote in 2015. As Fr Michael Collins said at the mass, 'He was one of our country's giants.'

Michael was a warm, gentle giant. As a world-leading paediatric ophthalmologist, he guided many parents and children through traumatic life experiences. Knowing we were running on a shoestring budget at Vision Sports Ireland, he put his hand in his own pocket and called his extensive network of friends to support us in reaching many more b/vi people.

Michael O'Keeffe grew up in Ballylough, Mitchelstown, in east Cork. His dad, Tom, was heavily involved in a co-operative movement, with the co-operative now known as Dairygold. His older brother Ned is a former Minister of State for Agriculture and Food.

In his early years Michael was a dedicated handball player who won two All-Ireland titles. He was known to be a fiercely competitive tennis player.

His incredible medical career began at UCC and then on to St Finbarr's, Cork, where he met his future wife, Eleanor. His ophthalmology career began in earnest in London, later bringing him to Dundee, Scotland, and Toronto, Canada.

In 1986 Michael was interviewed for a vacant position in ophthalmology at Dublin's Temple Street and the Mater hospitals. When asked by the interview panel what he would suggest being done with Temple Street, he said he'd bulldoze it! They gave him the job. Michael soon became well-known outside paediatrics for his trailblazing laser treatment, restoring failing sight to thousands of patients over the years.

As Jack Charlton's 'Put 'em under pressure' echoed throughout the land in June 1990, my wife Grainne and I were already under pressure. Our newly-born first child, Claire, was diagnosed by Michael as having cataracts blocking vision in both eyes. A fortnight after her birth, Michael zapped the cataracts from one eye, and shortly afterwards he operated on her other tiny eye.

Michael was our ray of light and hope at a difficult time for Grainne and me. His warm and kind manner of communication blew us away, as we were both used to the often-brash manner of old-school eye doctors.

Over the following years, I met Michael hundreds of times as he took care of our four children, as well as Grainne and me. He was always the gent who took time out for a chat and advice.

At his funeral mass, when Grainne and I heard Michael's friend Prof. Robert Acheson recall Christmas Eve O'Keeffe/ Acheson family gatherings and the infamous Dundee cocktails that were served, we had to laugh. You see, at Christmas 1992, Grainne was Michael's emergency in-patient at the Mater. We met him Christmas Eve and Christmas Day. Then, on the third day, Robert Acheson and Michael arrived to conduct a three-hour emergency procedure. Those Christmas Eve infamous Dundee cocktails must have been good, as the operation had some success.

Michael did countless favours for me and my family over the years and would never accept a return. I did, however, manage a kind of return.

In the summer of 2018 I received an invite from the British Embassy to attend a VIP garden party. As the event clashed with a family holiday, I had no hesitation in deciding it was the sun for me, not a rainy day in Dublin 4. By luck, Grainne asked me about the invite and immediately said, 'That's Harry and Meghan's garden party.'

I thought of Michael, confirmed his availability, and arranged for the embassy to switch my non-transferrable invite.

A fortnight later I bumped into Michael. 'Did you meet the Royals?' I asked. 'No,' he said, 'I was too busy at the back having a royal time with Magner and JP!'

His love of sports for blind and vision-impaired people goes back three decades. He was my guest at the opening of the European Games for the Blind at Belfield in 1993. He regularly sought updates on how b/vi sport was progressing.

In 2014 the Vision Sports Ireland board, of which I was a member, were anxious to find a new president to succeed the late Colm Murray. Encouraged by board member Róisín Dermody, I suggested Michael. Immediately and unanimously, the board agreed. Weeks later, board chairperson Robert Dobbyn and I trotted over to Temple Steet, where Michael was delighted to accept our invite.

Michael was always available to Vision Sports Ireland. Members fondly remember him for his lunchtime presentations at our annual Mayfests. Each year, he arrived with one of his many celebrity friends, including Derek Mooney, the late Mícheál Ó Muircheartaigh and Bláthnaid Ní Chofaigh. For our 2021 40th anniversary, he brought in Miriam O'Callaghan to host the closing ceremony for our online event.

He made several strong speeches at Vision Sports Ireland events over the years, all of which hit the nail on the head concerning the lack of public and big corporation funding. Never shy of controversy when he saw injustice, he wouldn't just tell you, he'd tell the nation on radio and TV.

I love the story Michael's son Nick tells of his dad and himself being turned away from a restaurant as they didn't have a booking. Michael told his son that the restaurant had it all wrong. He runs his practice and never turns anyone away.

Michael O'Keeffe, legend, has left us physically, but he's with us every day, everywhere.

35. Girls' talk

Women in sport including Greta Streimikyte (Dublin/Lithuania), Orla Comerford (Dublin), Babs Weiberg (Louth/Germany), Sinead Kane (Cork), Hilary Devlin (Dublin) and Róisín Dermody (Carlow).

If you can't see it, you can be it. Or, as world-beating blind golfer Jan Dinsdale MBE, 'putts' it, 'You don't need to see it to tee it!'

In September 2004, at the Canadian Blind Golf Open, Jan became the first blind golfer to get a hole-in-one.

The most popular sports among b/vi people – athletics, swimming, cycling, walking and tennis – are sports where males and females compete in the same arenas and where if you watch the men's competition, you'll watch the women's competition and vice-versa.

Arguably, Irish b/vi female athletes are more successful than the boys in elite sport. Three of Ireland's four Paralympic gold medallists are female; Northern Ireland's Kelly Gallagher won Great Britain's first-ever Winter Paralympics gold.

Yes, the girls beat the boys hands-down in most elite sports. Yet, research findings at grassroots level are not as rosy. In 2023 Vision Sports Ireland undertook a research project in partnership with Dublin City University (DCU) to determine baseline physical literacy and fundamental movement skills in teenage girls aged between ten and seventeen. Preliminary results from the first stage suggest girls who are b/vi may already be at a disadvantage in maintaining a healthy lifestyle due to reduced confidence and lower participation in sport and physical activity.

Only one in two participants were categorised as having a 'healthy' VO2 max score, with more than double the number of females categorised as 'at a health risk' for cardio-respiratory endurance compared to their male counterparts. We can only hope the success of our elite women will filter down to all levels sooner rather than later.

The move from print to online media has proven positive for women, not least in para-sports, where women account for 65 per cent of photo coverage. It's time for us to look up and be influenced by Ireland's talented b/vi female athletes.

Greta Streimikyte is a two-time European 1500m athletics champion who is about to represent Ireland in her third Paralympic Games. At fifteen, Greta moved to Ireland from Vilnius in Lithuania and attended Rosmini Community School in Drumcondra. Her PE teacher, Sean Gallagher, spotted her middle-distance talent and encouraged her to kick on. She is one of a set of triplets, born prematurely, and she contracted retinopathy, which now places her in the B3/T13 eyesight category for sport.

Greta, whose club is Clonliffe Harriers, is the European T13 1500m record holder.

Babs Weiberg is an untouchable Ireland vi tennis international since she took to the courts in October 2018.

From Hamburg, Germany, it was a hospital stay in Frankfurt in 1995 that converted her to what she calls 'my Ireland'. She explains, 'The lady in the next bed introduced me to her Cork family. They were stone-nuts, crazy, I loved them.' Five years later, Babs set up home in Ireland's north-east.

A year later, her Type 1 diabetes triggered diabetic retinopathy and macular degeneration. After getting over the shock, she took to walking and cycling, and she climbed Ben Nevis in Scotland.

Since her 2019 debut in Spain, she has successfully represented Ireland at several b/vi international tournaments and two world championships. She achieved a bronze medal at the 2023 competition in Poland.

Orla Comerford is a double IPC European sprint bronze medal winner who will compete in her third consecutive Paralympic Games in Paris in 2024. Orla joined Raheny Shamrocks athletics club at age six. At eleven, she was diagnosed with a degenerative condition, Stargardt disease, which affects her central vision.

At eighteen, she competed in her first Paralympic Games in Rio, reaching the final at T13 100m.

At the 2023 IPC World Championships, she knocked over half a second off her Rio 100m time with a personal best time of 12.14 seconds.

Along with Paralympic colleagues Katie-George Dunlevy, Greta Streimikyte and Peter Ryan, Orla is an ambassador for Fighting Blindness, the customer-led research, support and advocacy charity.

Hilary Devlin, Eye Clinic Liaison Officer (ECLO) at Vision Ireland, has an infectious love of sport, which knocks out her fellow staff and the dozens of parents, guardians and children she meets daily.

'Vision Sports and ECLO are the two best Vision Ireland services. I can't do my work without Vision Sports.' Hilary was the chairperson of Vision Sports Ireland two decades ago.

Hilary has sailed since she was six, trampolined through college, discus-thrown and ran and won the b/vi section of the Women's Mini Marathon. Now, she is a leading vi rugby player on the recently formed IRFU Old Wesley/Vision Sports Ireland team.

Róisín Dermody holds a place in Vision Sports Ireland history as the only child at the founding of the national governing body in November 1988. Three years later, she qualified for the Barcelona Paralympic Games, but it was not to be.

'I was born with the eye condition coloboma. Just as I moved to secondary school in my native Carlow, I had a detached retina. School went out the window, and so did my Paralympic journey.'

A lifelong swimmer, our water baby won dozens of awards, including five gold and two silver medals over seven years at the National Community Games under-16 handicapped swim event.

A young retiree from competition swimming, Róisín took to mountain skiing, water-skiing, rowing and, more recently, vi tennis. She returned to competition for the first two world tennis championships in Spain and Ireland.

Róisín supported Denis Toomey in founding the Irish Tandem Club and has served on the Irish Paralympic Council and joined the board of Vision Sports Ireland.

Sinead Kane is an ultra-runner extraordinaire from Youghal, Co. Cork. Her eye condition is aniridia, the absence of the coloured part of her eyes. She has 5 per cent vision.

Five years after running her first 10k at age thirty, she entered the *Guinness Book of Records* in 2017 for being the first visually impaired person to complete a marathon on each of the seven continents within seven days. A year later, she recorded the furthest distance for a female on a treadmill in twelve hours – another Guinness World Record.

Since 2019 Sinead has represented Ireland four times, including the IAU World and European 24-Hour Championships.

Other noteworthy high-performing female sportspeople include Nadine Lattimore, Liz Harold and Ailish Dunne (field events), Joan White (middle-distance running) and Carol Brill (golf).

36. Knock, knock, knockin' on Kevin's door

Blind football with player Kevin Kelly (Donegal) and manager Alex Whelan (Dublin).

Kevin Kelly will never forget his last GAA game.

'It was an under-12s football semi-final in Donegal with my local club Urris. With less than twelve minutes remaining, I came on. We were losing when I caught the ball and kicked it high up into the air. It dipped under the bar, goal! Then the keeper kicked it out again, and it landed in my hands. Sure, why not try the same kick again? This time, it hit the top of the bar and over for a point. Game over, we won!'

Shortly afterwards, Kevin had retinal detachment and lost his sight in one eye. Almost eighteen months later, at age fourteen, Kevin's other eye blurred.

'My consultant, Peter Barry, carried out a procedure which was unsuccessful. He called my parents and myself into a room where he said he was willing to operate again, but the outcome may be like what happened with my first eye. I was upset and saw no point in further procedures.'

Kevin eventually relented, but sadly, there was no stopping the sight loss. He was diagnosed with Stickler syndrome, a hereditary condition where the connective tissue weakens, so every time they reattached the retina, the weakened tissue would reject it.

But, ten years after his first sight loss and last football match, he was back scoring goals again.

'My then-girlfriend, now wife, Christina, saw a post on Facebook for a come-and-try session for blind football in Tralee, Co. Kerry. I wasn't interested, but she persuaded me, saying we could make a weekend of it, and we could drop in on the football session.' The rest is history, as Kevin loved the game and has gone on to represent Ireland eight times to date.

Irish blind football manager Alex Whelan explains, 'The game is played with modified FIFA rules. The field of play is smaller, surrounded by fibreglass boards and looks like a narrow five-a-side astro pitch.

'Teams consist of four outfield totally blind players with a fully-sighted goalkeeper. To ensure fair competition, all outfield players must wear eyeshades.

'Outside the pitch, there's an attack coach who can only give direction for the final third of the pitch. The head coach takes care of the midfield third, while the goalkeeper takes care of the defence third. It is an offence for any coach to direct players outside their remit.

'Before attempting to tackle, players must shout the word 'Voy' so that the person they are attempting to tackle is aware. This rule is critical, and any player who breaks it will be penalised. Any player who breaks the rule five times gets a red card.

'The ball is equipped with a noise-making device to allow players to locate it by sound. The game is played to the sound of silence.

'Matches consist of two fifteen-minute halves, with a ten-minute break at half-time.

'Before each game, players warm up, concentrating on orientation. Players walk/run a few laps of the pitch to build spatial awareness by calculating the length, width and feel of the pitch, step counting all the way.'

Alex Whelan has the highly sought-after UEFA B coaching licence. He grew up in Ballymun, where his favourite sports were boxing, tennis, karate and 'everything else going on in the estate, including kiss chasing!

'Soccer was number one. I tried GAA but couldn't pick the ball up and scored more goals than points.'

Alex's mum, Claire Whelan, lost her sight through retinitis pigmentosa (RP) in her mid-thirties. In recent years, she has joined in all the fun of sports. In 2017 she represented Ireland at VI Tennis in Spain.

While Alex was familiar with many activities involving b/vi people, he had never heard of blind football until 2012.

'In 2012 my local club, Ballymun United, hosted a blind football training session. I was invited along as they were short of coaches. I dropped by more out of curiosity. How could blind people play football? What I saw conquered me. I was smitten and fell in love with it straight away.

'It was a one-off game, and I heard no more until the coach who invited me along called me to say, "The players haven't stopped talking about you, Alex. They want you back." That was music to my ears. I was on the first bus down to the next session.

'I always see blind footballers as players, never seeing disability. Some coaches are patronising, saying, "Isn't Johnny great for trying when you consider his lack of sight?" That's not my way. Players want to be pushed, be the best, and I'm there to encourage and eff them out of it, although sometimes they eff me out of it, too. Ultimately, we share respect.'

After gelling as a team, they travelled to play England at RNC Hereford. 'We knew we were up against it,' recalls Alex, 'So, we got everyone behind the ball, conceded three penalties, but somehow earned a draw, totally against the run of play.'

Four years later, the FAI awarded the Irish team international status. Alex remembers travelling through Dublin Airport en route to the IBSA European qualifiers in Romania. 'As we didn't have enough guides, we moved together as a walking train. Each player had his hand on the shoulder of the individual ahead. For the first time, we had our official Irish tracksuits. What a sight, what a feeling, we were so proud.'

Ireland finished fifth of eight in the qualifiers. Later that year, they drew with the highly rated Belgium and beat Hungary.

A year later, the Ireland blind football team achieved their greatest-ever result at the IBSA Challenge Cup in Krakow. They reached the final where they narrowly lost out to hosts Poland.

Alex is a top world coach who trained with world champions Brazil in 2019.

In May 2024, following a long Covid-driven break, the Ireland blind football team returned to international competition, to RNC Hereford where it all began eleven years earlier.

Blind football is not a game for the faint-hearted. He says, 'In contact sport, your chance of injury is multiplied. Players will shoulder each other, tackle hard, may clash, or lose concentration and orientation. It's a fast and furious game.'

Kevin Kelly agrees. 'It's kind of a cross between soccer and Gaelic football. It's more physical than your average game of soccer, with the cut and thrust of GAA. Communication is key.

'Sports such as blind football has the added benefit of helping totally blind people when out and about trying to navigate street corners. Your confidence is higher. You're more alert and paying attention to your environment.'

The sport is the only football game at Paralympic Games. Women's blind football will be introduced for LA 2028.

Kevin has the last word. 'Whether you're b/vi, parent, relative, friend, educator or elsewhere in the game, you must try out football. You can play recreationally at club level, and maybe internationally. It's suitable for all ages, male and female. And you are guaranteed to make friends for life.'

37. With a little help from our friends

Volunteers, guides, pilots, drivers.

Two to tango, two to tandem. In b/vi sport, it takes two, baby, maybe more.

At the 2009 Irish Blind Golf Captain's Dinner, former RTÉ Radio Head of Sport and blind golfer Ian Corr described guides as 'the extra club in the bag'.

Blind golfer Dermot Bolger explains it so well in his tribute poem:

> *'Whether we call them lovers, partners, sighted coaches, or friends,*
> *Our only certainty is our need for someone in whom we place our faith.*
> *So read the grain of greens for me, reassure me about how my ball lies,*
> *Alert me to bunkers, to what is within my range or what is out of bounds.'*

Our first blind marathoner, Jimmy Gallagher, was never shy in finding opportunities to acknowledge his sighted running partners. His first guide was a legend himself, a top Irish amateur and pro boxer called Liam 'Ski' Mullen. When Ski retired from boxing, he returned to the army and worked with Jimmy, who was a telephonist in St Bricin's military hospital beside Dublin's Phoenix Park.

Five decades ago, I arranged an interview for Jimmy on a prime-time Irish radio programme presented by RTÉ's Mike Murphy. Jimmy turned up with Ski and said he would only do the live interview if Ski could join him. The producer explained there was only one guest studio seat, and it was for Jimmy only. Jimmy refused and walked away. An angry Jimmy and an angry producer both rang me. Somehow, it was sorted, and Jimmy, Ski and Mike Murphy settled into a lively radio chat.

While Ski ran with Jimmy everywhere for three decades, Declan Smyth piloted him in his later years. Jimmy would never sign off on an interview without crediting Ski and Declan.

Many athletes, including Gerry Campbell, Carol Carr and Bridie Lynch, single out one very special man – my coach, the late Eddie Hogan.

Eddie's heart lay in Donore Harriers, now based in Dublin's Chapelizod. In the 1950s and 60s, he coached Donore teams to an unprecedented sixteen consecutive national cross-country championships. He also coached at least ten Olympians and advised many more, including world record indoor miler and 1983 world 5000m champion Eamonn Coghlan.

Eddie believed in me more than I believed in myself. We were always together in the 80s until his passing. He loved b/vi athletics and was there for all involved, although he would never accept offers to manage our international teams.

Absolutely every athlete from the early days mentions Anne Kielty, our manager from 1981 to 1984. Anne had boundless energy and enthusiasm and is so warmly remembered by all who knew her.

Atlanta '96 sole gold medallist Bridie Lynch thanks her teammates Gerry Campbell and Catherine Walsh for helping to make it happen. In common with her fellow Paralympian Fintan

O'Donnell, she also singles out coaches Eamonn Harvey, John Davis and Tony Guest for special mentions. Those three names are mentioned by so many.

Paralympian Gus Dorrington credits running mate and mentor Eddie Lynch for keeping him in athletics. 'One time, I was two minutes late in meeting him for a training session. "What do you mean being late? I'm here freezing my balls off waiting."' Gus was never late again.

Fighting Blindness CEO Finbarr Roche says, 'When I was asked to join the board of Vision Sports Ireland, I was honoured. The impact it has had on the health and well-being of generations of blind and vision-impaired people is inestimable and has ensured the success of the organisation.

'The dedication of the participants and volunteers is remarkable, often travelling several hours to compete, guide or spectate, such is the rarity of accessible sport in their locality, which bears testament to the inclusive ethos and camaraderie instilled at all levels. Events that leave an indelible mark on my memory include our early participation in parkrun, Mayfest and winning charity of choice for the Galway Cycle run by NUI Maynooth.

'It would be remiss of me not to mention the outstanding voluntary board of the time and particularly our president, Prof. Michael O'Keeffe, whose dedication to the charity and his patients left a massive impression upon me. He is a huge loss to the community.

'It became clear to me early on that Joe Geraghty, having founded the organisation with others in 1979, is the beating heart of the space and possesses an encyclopaedic knowledge of events and people spanning many decades. His contribution cannot be understated. He has been the driving force of the organisation for many years,' Finbarr Roche concludes.

Triple-gold Paralympian Katie-George Dunlevy pays tribute to her tandem pilot Eve McCrystal, 'It's a team sport. I'm so grateful to Eve for her commitment over the years and her ability to race. I respect Eve's dedication and ability to be a successful sportswoman while juggling a young family and a career. We have great respect and trust in each other.'

In the past two years, Katie-G has been working with pilot Linda Kelly. 'It's tricky finding a compatible pilot,' adds Katie. 'Like Eve, Linda is determined and committed, one of the best cyclists in Ireland. Our pilots make many sacrifices and give so much time to the sport. I really appreciate all the effort.'

In 2023 Linda Kelly piloted Katie as they won two gold medals at the UCI Para-cycle World Championships in Scotland.

Elite para-triathlete Donnacha McCarthy agrees, 'A tandem is a more difficult machine to handle than your ordinary race bike. As a totally blind athlete, the guide must be my eyes while training and racing as we cycle, lake swim and run. However, the guide also needs to be with me before and after all activities. It's a massive commitment but rewarding. Dave Tilley took me to an elite para-triathlon. Sean Husband is with me on the road to Paris '24.'

When Bob Auerbach's sight faded over two decades ago, he gave up his high-powered motorcycle for a push bike. While taking a break from his telephony role at Dun Laoghaire Rathdown County Council, he got chatting with their architect Dominic Coyle. Dominic later asked if he might substitute the bike for a tandem ride in Dublin's Phoenix Park. 'Will I f***!' beamed Bob. The boys have been inseparable ever since and regularly attend tandem gatherings from Maynooth to Mayfest and Dublin to Dundalk.

Pioneer Paralympian Pat Kelly says, 'We all need a support network. For b/vi athletes, particularly those with no sight, we need that extra support around us. To guide, drive from A to B, coach us in specifics we can't see, assist at events, and fill many gaps. We are so grateful to all who support us.'

Pat mentions many names, but three stick out for me: Jack Bracken, and Anne and Jimmy Kelly.

Anne and Jimmy Kelly were amazing. For many years, they volunteered wherever they could find b/vi sportspeople. They drove minibuses, made the best sandwiches and ensured everyone was taken care of. Their son John represented Ireland at the 1984 Paralympics and later chaired Vision Sports Ireland. Following Jimmy's passing in 2023, I was chatting with Anne, and I was thanking her for all Jimmy and she had done for us. Anne replied, 'It was worth every minute, Joe. Only the other day, we were saying how those 1993 Euros in Dublin were the best experience of our lives.'

Jack Bracken was a care worker with ChildVision and began his links with b/vi sport in the early 1980s. He cajoled and inspired many pupils into football, athletics, swimming, tandem cycling, horse-riding and judo. He travelled as an official with many of our teams abroad and was our deputy manager at the '84 Paralympics. With colleagues Mary Leonard and Brian Allen, he hosted hundreds of our Mayfest overseas guests at ChildVision.

Surely the most dedicated Mayfest supporters over five decades must be Lughaith O'Modhrain and his guide and family friend Colm O'Suileabhan. Each year Colm takes time out to fly home from his Swiss base to guide Lughaith through multiple sports. Theirs is a unique bond.

We can't leave Mayfest without credit to Kate and Robert Dobbyn, who took on the management of the games in the early noughties. Ever since, they pop up each year with two dozen or more schoolgirl volunteers from the Dublin secondary school at Mount Anville. Robert joined the board at Vision Sports Ireland and was chair from 2013 to 2016.

The gift of volunteering often passes from generation to generation. Paralympics Ireland vice president and pioneering tandem pilot Denis Toomey got his gift of the give from his parents. 'I was born into Cork GAA, where my dad was a player, inter-county referee and chair, secretary and treasurer at various times of our hometown Mitchelstown GAA Club. My mum was a camogie player who trained our local team.

'As a teen, I joined the Red Cross, where I have volunteered for over fifty years and served as Cork area secretary and on Central Council. My parents ensured volunteering was instilled in me from an early age.'

From GAA, Denis joined the early 1980s marathon-running craze before injury steered him into cycling. On a Co-Operation North Maracycle – a weekend 300-km round-trip cycle linking the cities of Dublin and Belfast – he noticed a promotion for Blazing Saddles, Vision Ireland's cycling fundraiser led by Eamon Duffy. Later, he signed up for their 1994 Sydney to Brisbane Cycle. He watched ten b/vi people cycle tandems, and he was hooked.

'Australia was my first encounter with b/vi people. Eamon Duffy had the incredibly innovative idea that we should each spend an evening looking after a visually impaired person. Geraldine Looney was assigned to me. I learned so much from Geraldine and was blown away. How visually impaired people get on with their lives and where the barriers are. It showed me how people with disabilities can participate in sport at quite an elevated level.'

Five years later, Denis cycled in Thailand with former showband star Joe Bollard. A year later, they were US-bound, as they joined a Blazing Saddles team led by Tour de France legend Sean Kelly. RTÉ TV recorded a very enjoyable and educational set of programmes.

Denis Toomey then founded Tandem Cycling Ireland with a view to cycling at the 2004 Paralympic Games. 'I thought this would be easy: Get an entry form and sign up.' Multiple globetrotting qualifying events later, Ireland qualified one bike for Athens.

Mark Kehoe has the honour of being Ireland's first paracyclist. Denis piloted him on road, while Ian Mahon led on the track. Banbridge legend Gerry Beggs managed an all-volunteer team to nineteenth overall of thirty-four countries.

From 2001 to 2022, Denis organised the Mayfest cycle over 10- and 20-mile routes. This hugely popular event attracted cyclists of many disabilities who were eager to qualify for competitions, including the Paralympic Games.

In 2013 Denis became president of Cycling Ireland. Three years later, he was chef de mission at the Rio Paralympics. A year later, he topped the poll in elections to the Olympic Federations of Ireland.

Denis Toomey joins the list of so many who unselfishly lend a hand to support b/vi people overcome blocks to living a fuller life.

38. Fields of gold

Multi-sport with Wally Roode (Dublin/South Africa), including athletics, blind golf, cricket, para-triathlon, parkrun, rugby and wrestling.

Born into fields of gold in eastern South Africa, Willem 'Wally' Roode has done it all. He's a talented multi-sportsman who has represented Ireland in futsal, blind golf and tennis.

Wally's dad was an industrial electrician operating out of the South African goldmines. Both of his grandads worked in the mines. Sadly, his maternal grandad died in a mining accident.

Wally's parents were aware of his poor vision, but it wasn't a problem around the house. At his local primary school, he could see little of what was happening in class, so he moved school and boarded at Prinshof School for Visually Impaired in Pretoria.

'I spent thirteen years there,' recalls Wally. 'We had great sports facilities, including an eight-lane 25-metre pool, sports halls, and sports fields. We had everything. I never walked, just ran. My mum said I had ants in my pants.

'My number-one sport was wrestling. I was physically strong. I'm as round as I am thick. I became Northern Transvaal Provincial Champion.'

B/vi people have taken to the wrestling rings for almost 200 years. It had its grounding in US and European blind schools in the 1840s. Several have competed for national titles. In 1933,

John Johnston, a blind innkeeper from Stamfordham, England, competed in the world championships (able-bodied).

On 20 October 2018, Jordan Percy (then thirteen) made Irish wrestling history as he became the first-ever visually impaired person to win a medal – silver – at the Irish Open Wrestling Championships. (Just so you know, Jordan's mum, Tracey, is the most infectious advocate for b/vi sport you will ever meet.)

While Wally Roode was educated during the apartheid era at a white-only school, he had good connections with the non-white population. No doubt, he was strongly influenced by his dad, whose mining work kept him in contact with all races and creeds.

'Sport was mixed,' says Wally. 'I had great competition in swimming and athletics. I remember the year I broke the South African b/vi 100m athletics record with a time of 11.4 seconds. I was racing against a non-white guy, and I dipped on the line.'

Wally enjoyed the competition and camaraderie in mixed sport.

After leaving school, he was conscripted into the army. 'After a month or so at the army base, they called us out for sight-testing. I was standing in the queue, and I said to the guy in front of me, "Tell me the letters, tell me the letters!" So, he told me, and I remembered the letters down to the second last line. My time came, and the sergeant said, "Right, son, close one eye and start reading the chart from the bottom up." No chance. He immediately said, "Well, we won't be giving you a gun!"'

Exempted from the army – although offered a desk job – his next stop was the North London School of Physiotherapy. The college was on the grounds of the Whittington Hospital, called after Sir Richard Whittington, the man who inspired the tale of Dick Whittington and his cat. No felines for Wally, but he had feelings for a female. He found his future wife, the seven-times Irish Paralympian Catherine Walsh.

Sport was all around at college. 'We played rugby in winter and cricket in the summer. My partially sighted friend and I played on a mainstream rugby team as props. We could play the physical side, push for tries. Our teammates knew we couldn't see much, so they helped us out, and we helped them. Later, when I set up home in Ireland in 1996, I played rugby with Skerries Rugby Club's second and third teams. I won a Leinster medal with the third team. I played a game on the first team when they were totally stuck.

'In the summertime, while I was in London, we played b/vi cricket. I was a member of the Metro Blind Sport Club. There were four or five teams in London and many more around the UK. We played in a league where the two top teams played a final test at Lords. I played in finals at Lords from '92 to '94 and once played in a televised demo there when England were hosting Pakistan in a five-day test.'

Vision sight classification for blind cricket relies on visual acuity and does not require field vision measurements for competition. Participants may play in two categories: Class One is for those with visual acuity equivalent to B1, while Class Two is for cricketers with visual acuity covered by B2/B3.

In 1997 Wally represented his adopted country, Ireland, at the European Futsal Championships in Barcelona.

Wally always wanted to play golf. He took to blind golf like a duck to a water bunker and represented Ireland at four world championships. He won three Irish Blind Golf opens.

Before winning his last Irish golf open in 2018, Wally won bronze at the world b/vi tennis championships in Shankill, Dublin.

'Tennis was another game I always wanted to play. I tried lawn tennis, but the ball was too fast to see. Vi tennis is different.'

Wally has competed in up to thirty triathlons, and ten years ago, he won silver in the Irish national para-triathlon championships. He believes in mixing sport and, with his physiotherapist hat on, advises against too much running: 'Think of what your body may be like when you are older.'

He's a fan of parkruns as 'they're short and sweet'.

Parkrun Ireland is an active supporter of b/vi walking and running. Prompted by an RTÉ TV *Operation Transformation* programme featuring Vision Sports Ireland, Joan Ryan led the charge to recruit b/vi people into parkruns. Each Saturday – Sunday for the juniors – dozens of b/vi people participate in free-to-enter 5k parkruns throughout Ireland with active support from volunteer guides and officials.

Just like Wally Roode, I recommend parkruns. They get your weekends buzzing from the half-hour jog to the coffee afterwards.

39. Let's hear it for the boys

Men in sport, including Fintan O'Donnell (Limerick), Conal McNamara (Mayo), Mick Clarke (Meath), James Brown (Down), Donnacha McCarthy (Cork) and Tony Ward (Monaghan).

Was it a cheetah, was it a comet? Oh no, it's the 'Kildimo Kid' himself, Fintan O'Donnell from Limerick, racing over the finish line to win bronze at Paralympics '84 in New York. Having never run 800m before, Fintan split the finishing tape in two minutes and two seconds.

'Quite a special day,' recalls Fintan. 'Leading up, I broke our Irish record in heat one, and my teammate, John Kelly, smashed my record in heat two. We both qualified for the final, and I broke John's record again. I can remember little except it was a fast first half, and on the final 200m, I began my sprint to the line.'

Fintan and I have a little sympathy for John Kelly. A few days earlier, John and I ran in the 1500m heats. John broke the Irish record in heat one, and I broke it minutes later in heat two.

Fintan has aniridia, part of a syndrome where he was born with congenital cataracts and glaucoma. With no iris, he is susceptible to glare and bright lights.

From mainstream schooling to St Joseph's, he began to enjoy many sports. Re-integrating into the mainstream at second level, his choice of sport was reduced. 'The hurling and football at my new school at Pallaskenry, Co. Limerick, were too fast, but I could run cross-country and do athletics.'

Following his Paralympic glory in athletics, Fintan trained as a physiotherapist in London and took on new sporting challenges, including kayaking and skiing.

After his tireless voluntary physiotherapy endeavours at the Dublin Euro Championships in 1993, he joined the board of Vision Sports Ireland, where he later became chairperson. He was the official Paralympics Ireland Irish lead team physio at Athens, Beijing and London. He is the chairperson of the PI National Classification Committee. As if that wasn't enough, Fintan is the anti-doping officer at Vision Sports Ireland.

In May 2021 Fintan O'Donnell was inducted into the Vision Sports Ireland Hall of Fame.

At sweet sixteen, Conal McNamara (Mayo) was running fifty-second 400m track races for fun. He ranks sixth on the all-time b/vi Paralympics medals table, having won silver in Athens in 2004. The previous year, he won a European silver medal and competed at the World Championships. The ever-popular Conal then turned his extraordinary talent to music and communications.

James Brown (Down) is the most talented b/vi middle-distance athlete I have met. I first met him at the Rotary Stoke Mandeville Games in June 1982. We immediately hit it off, and I almost convinced him to run for Ireland.

I ran against James in the 1984 Paralympic Games, where he won double gold for Great Britain at 800m and 1500m. Twenty-eight years later, he returned for London 2012, winning bronze for Ireland in the tandem time trial with pilot Michael Shaw.

Four years later, he was banned for thirty months by Sport Ireland for doping violations. Next, we heard of James in 2019, when he glued himself to a jet at London City Airport to campaign for action on climate change. A small stint as a guest of Her Majesty's followed.

James is so passionate and talented that there is no knowing where he'll put his energies next.

Tony Ward (Monaghan) is one of the best-known b/vi people in the general disability advocacy field. What is less known is that he was an accomplished athlete who twenty-three years ago won a bronze medal at the European Cross-Country Championships for b/vi people. With colleague Neil O'Donovan, he was a key player in the immediate post-millennium organisation of sport for b/vi people here and was also chairperson of Vision Sports Ireland.

Mick Clarke (Meath) came to Vision Sports Ireland in 1989 as a top mainstream national cross-country runner. He has had thirteen international call-ups, including a marathon bronze medal at the 1993 Euro games in Dublin. Mick is a three-time Paralympian who has served on the board of Paralympics Ireland. He was also chairperson of Vision Sports Ireland and led its rebranding in 2013.

In May 2015 Mick Clarke was inducted into the Vision Sports Ireland Hall of Fame.

In 2017 Eamonn Tilley, high-performance para-triathlon coach, first met Donnacha McCarthy (Cork).

Eamonn asked, 'What's your 750m swim time? To which Donnacha replied, 'Don't have one.' In fact, Donnacha could only swim half the length of an indoor pool back then.

Eamonn asked, 'Your bike time?' To which Donnacha replied, 'Don't have one.'

Eamonn asked, 'And your 5km run time?' Donnacha replied, 'Don't have one.'

So, how many national titles has Donnacha won since then? He can't say 'Don't have one' as he has won five and counting.

Aged six, Donnacha developed leukaemia in his bone marrow, underwent chemotherapy, and, after four years of remission, it returned to his spine. He was diagnosed with optic neuropathy due to acute lymphatic leukaemia. He went from 20/20 vision to zero in six weeks.

Donnacha received massive support from his family and school and managed to cycle with his sister running alongside him, as well as being encouraged to participate in school sports.

After moving from his rural west Cork home to UCC, Donnacha heard of Vision Sports Ireland and the FAI Football for All programme with their top coach, Nick Harrison. He attended a taster session for blind football. He says, 'It lit a spark. Nick was so supportive. I fell back in love with sport. The next day, I had aches all over, and I knew I was back.'

Four years later, Donnacha McCarthy captained the Irish blind football team on their successful European tournaments in Romania and Poland. 'I scored my first-ever goal in Romania. That's a huge highlight for me. Also, as a kid, I dreamed of putting on the Ireland jersey. It's funny but losing my sight gave me that opportunity years later. A huge honour.'

To complement his football, Donnacha took to running with Crusaders Athletics Club in Dublin. Some days, he jogged out with his work colleagues at Vodafone Ireland. A decade ago, Vodafone was Triathlon Ireland's sponsor. While on a lunchtime run, a friend suggested he attend a para-triathlon taster day with her coach, Eamonn Tilley. So, from zero to hero, with Eamonn leading the way.

Finding a regular guide is always a challenge. Eamonn's brother Dave stepped in. 'He was brilliant,' says Donnacha. 'He was more than a guide and got me out on days when I could have stayed in bed.'

In 2018, guided by Dave, Donnacha became the first blind person in Ireland to complete Dublin's Liffey Swim.

Donnacha now had his sights set on Tokyo 2020. Dave stepped aside to make way for a variety of guides, including Brian McCrystal. Tokyo came and passed as Donnacha missed out by the cruellest of margins. In September 2021 Sean Husband took control of guiding, and Donnacha, with the support of Triathlon Ireland, reached new highs on the road to Paris '24.

There are so many highly notable b/vi guys excelling in sport, including Peter Ryan, Damien Vereker and Martin Gordon (tandem cycling); Pádraig McLoughlin (various); Noel McInerney (marathon), Michael Keane (sprints); Michael Doyle and Robert McGee (judo); Ross Gallagher (parkruns); Pat Morgan Jnr and his dad, Pat Morgan Snr (blind golf) and Andrew FitzGerald (athletics and cycling).

40. What's another steer

Rally navigator Sara McFadden (Mayo), including camogie and rally navigation.

How would you like to race a rally car at 180 km/h guided by instruction from your vision-impaired navigator?

It's happening in rallies across Ireland right now as top drivers avail of the expertise of ace navigator Sara McFadden.

Sara, who has very little sight due to albinism and nystagmus (underdeveloped back-of-the-eye nerves) is the first-ever vision impaired person licenced to compete with Motorsport Ireland.

Sligo IT Business graduate Sara (twenty-three), from Castlebar in Mayo, is the eldest daughter of rally icons Keith and Sandra McFadden. Her baby sister, Vanessa (eighteen), is next on the starting grid. While Sara's drive is rallying, she is into all sports and represented Mayo at an underage All-Ireland camogie final.

'Sport is my way of life and all I was ever interested in,' Sara says. 'I played every sport under the sun, including soccer and GAA. I was also strongly influenced by my cousin Kelly Gallagher who won Paralympic gold for Great Britain at alpine skiing in Sochi in 2014.

'One day at school, the hurling coach came in. I was hooked and joined the club straight away. Later, when I was thirteen, I got my first trial for Mayo playing camogie and was accepted into the county squad.' Camogie is an Irish team sport where players use prescribed wooden sticks with a flat base at the end to hurl or puck a hard stitched leather ball, similar to but smaller than a baseball.

As Sara says, 'Camogie is not an obvious sport for someone with a vision impairment. I couldn't see the ball and listened out until it came very close. Following my marker also helped.'

Sara is a natural leader and captained the defeated Mayo under-14 team to the 2013 All-Ireland camogie final at Croke Park. She laughs as she recalls a later experience at county level as a goalkeeper.

'Our first and second goalkeepers were not available. We needed a goalkeeper, so, strangely, they asked me. I thought, *that's an interesting choice*, and asked, "Are you sure?" "Yeah, you have the best puck out." I couldn't argue with the coach, so I stood in. Game on, and the ball went wide, and I asked the umpire where the ball was. "Are you blind?" the umpire asked. "Yes, I am!" I retorted.'

The players were aware of Sara's poor sight, but the county coaches were surprised. Sara stayed with the team up to minor level (under-18s). She feels that in recent years, the introduction of easier-to-see yellow balls at county level – initially brought in for floodlit games – and a general inclusion atmosphere make it easier to play the game.

Despite the speed of the ball, Sara considered continuing with GAA, but most games were at weekends, when the McFadden family went rallying around Ireland.

'As a child, I was my dad's little helper, emptying his toolbox, washing the windscreen and being with him as he readied for the rally. The atmosphere was just so lovely. As a teenager, I accepted

I couldn't drive. The only other option was to navigate. It wasn't what I set out to do, but I did it. I'm now so glad to be doing it.'

Since her first race in 2018, Sara has competed in twenty-five Irish rallies. In February 2022 Motor Sport Ireland awarded her a prestigious place in their rally academy. The academy enables Sara to fully equip herself to navigate at European and World Championships.

'It's fantastic as I now have access to nutritionists and performance coaches. The coaching is interesting, where I focus on general fitness, core, strength and flexibility. The neck exercises are most important, as I can be sitting in a fixed position for hours at a time.'

Once the race calendar is issued each November, Sara agrees her five to seven new-year rally events.

Her race week begins with a paper mapping route review, which contains specific twist and turn-coded markings. By midweek, it's on to the route video reviews, usually liaising with her driver. Diet and nutrition balancing also come into play. By Friday, it's time to wrap up at the office as it's squeaky-bum time and the sports psychology kicks in. Saturday morning, it's route test-driving.

'It's our last opportunity to tweak our mapping,' explains Sara. 'Routes cannot change due to licencing and permits. However, a circuit start could be moved forward if there is a significant local event, such as a funeral. On our final route inspection, we make determinations on weather conditions, including possible floodings. On Irish country roads, we must also note accumulations of horse and cow shit!'

Sunday is racing day, and, for Sara, it's ten hours or so of total concentration, always preparing for the unexpected.

'My role is to provide directions strictly following our agreed mapping. The driver may see the first bend but may not be aware of what follows. I would direct three steps ahead.'

Her formulae are getting results. In 2019 she hit the podium on three separate occasions with glittering bronze.

Sara McFadden now works with Vision Sports Ireland as their Partnerships and Operations Co-ordinator and Women in Sport Lead.

No doubt she'll steer us to new levels.

41. New York state of mind

Blind golfer Paul McCormack (Donegal/USA).

'I was commanding officer of the 41st Precinct of the NYPD on 9/11,' recalls Paul McCormack. 'It was very frightening; we knew there was a terrorist attack, but finding out precisely what was going on was difficult amid the chaos and rumours.

'I sent two vanloads of cops down, but telecommunications went out, so I lost contact with them. It was the day that changed the world.'

Two thousand six hundred and six people were murdered when two hijacked jets crashed through the World Trade Center on 11 September 2001.

A day later Paul was wading through dust clouds and chemicals when his eyes began to burn. Despite medical treatment, his eyes blurred for several days. Six months later, Paul McCormack, the youngest ever NYPD captain, aged twenty-nine, discovered he was no longer one of the sharpest shooters in the NYPD. He was missing the bullseye in mandatory police target shooting tests. His sight was failing, triggered by the 9/11 aftermath.

Paul lost many colleagues and friends on that fateful day. His heart and soul are with them, their families and all who supported the rescue.

'When the towers were hit, civilians living close by left their pets behind. Our team escorted the civilians back. When we got to their homes, it was just awful. The impact of the aeroplanes crashing through the Twin Towers meant bodies and body parts were being found on close-by high-rise balconies. It's something you should never see. Everything stopped each time we discovered a body to enable us to honour and give dignity to innocent victims.'

Paul McCormack is a proud Donegal man born in Philadelphia to Donegal parents who emigrated to the United States in the 1950s. In the early '70s the family returned to Ballybofey.

Following a solid Donegal academic and sporting education, Paul and his brothers – there are seven in the family – found themselves back in the States. 'For farm boys from rural Donegal in the 1980s who didn't have a pot to piss in, there was no option but to leave Ireland.'

The youth of Donegal headed in their masses to New York and the emigrant Irish communities of the Bronx and Yonkers. Paul recalls, 'I was playing minor football for Donegal as well as Sean MacCumhaill's GAA Club in Ballybofey. The entire GAA club of that generation emigrated.'

After four years working construction, Paul joined the New York Police Department and soon helped set up the NYPD GAA Club, where he was chair for eleven years.

With failing sight after 9/11, he gave up the football for good. He also gave up golf for good, too – or so he thought!

'A few times a week, the Irish NYPD and Irish barmen would come off shift at four in the morning and head to the golf course. But then it became embarrassing as my friends would have to tell me where the ball was. I couldn't see it. I gave it up.'

Thirteen years later, having left his beloved NYPD, Paul returned to Ireland with his wife Nicola and young family. Soon, he found golf once more.

'Friends were playing in a fundraising outing and were short a player on the day. They invited me and offered to support me. I was hesitant and felt I'd slow them down. I played, knocking in a few pars amid the snowballs. The bug was back. I was introduced to Irish Blind Golf, and I haven't looked back.'

Paul has played and won in both the British and US Blind Golf Opens. He also played and won at two Vision Cups - the Ryder Cup of Blind Golf.

In the autumn of 2018 Paul McCormack's friend Paul O'Rahilly, a blind golf player and key administrator, told me of a proposal to hold the International Sports Promotion Society Handa Vision Cup in Dublin the following year. I immediately jumped on board and joined the two Pauls in organising. It was a juggernaut which almost derailed on several occasions. But, led by Paul McCormack, we got there in style.

Paul O'Rahilly explains: 'The Vision Cup was held at Portmarnock Links - where Paul McCormack is a member - in June 2019. The top twelve blind golfers from North America took on the top twelve from the Rest of the World. Each team consisted of four golfers from each of the sight categories.

'The proximity to the sea, strong winds, fast greens and deep rough made for a most difficult challenge. Captained by Garrett Slattery, the Rest of World team took home the Cup.'

Aside from the ISPS Handa sponsorship and endorsement, funding and support were generously provided by Vision Sports Ireland, Sport Ireland, Fingal County Council, Golfing Union of Ireland (now Golf Ireland) and the R&A, as well as local businesses.

Paul also organised some fundraising golf tournaments around the country.

Paul McCormack, with his charisma and boundless energy, was the tournament director. He demands perfection from himself, whether on the golf course or organising an event. He singlehandedly raised the bar for this blue-riband tournament for blind golf for others to follow.

Amid the fierce competition during Vision Cup Week, Paul O'Rahilly recalls, 'It was the multi-sport sampler day at Kinseally Golf Academy where the children touched everyone's hearts – encouraging the next generation to participate in sport, regardless of their ability.'

Paul McCormack shares his friend's view on developing ability over disability. 'Being vision impaired can get you down, depressed, and have you feeling sad for yourself. I didn't realise there were outlets like blind golf and other b/vi sports. Some people think b/vi sport is a joke. Let me tell you, IT IS NOT!

'After sight loss, I never thought I could feel those competitive butterflies again. At the 2022 Vision Cup at TPC Sawgrass, home of the PGA Tour, my playing partner was Chad Nesmith, who is totally blind. He was hitting balls 250 yards down the pipe. Incredible. People can't fathom how difficult this is until they see it.'

All Paul is saying is, 'Give sport a chance. You may not be good at it, but it gets you out. You meet people, go for a pint, have the crack. Sports like golf are handicapped, where we all have an equal chance. Go for sport. You have absolutely nothing to lose.'

42. No matter how I tri

With para-triathlete Chloe MacCombe (Derry) and Eamonn Tilley (Dublin).

The February 2017 Paralympics Ireland talent-spotting expo at the Sport Ireland Indoor Arena was a quiet affair. As chairperson of Vision Sports Ireland, I took care of our stand with colleague Rahim Nazarali, and we had just a few callers.

So I took off on a lap of the brand-new track with Greta Streimikyte, watched by one spectator, Orla Comerford, Greta's teammate. I wasn't going to race Jason Smyth or cycle against the clock with Katie-George Dunlevy, so we all just chatted. I tried out some activities, but the talent-spotters didn't rate me. So, I sauntered over to the judo mats, where teenage twins Judith and Chloe MacCombe from Derry were throwing shapes.

On my shoulder was my good friend, the triathlon legend Eamonn Tilley. 'These girls are talented, Joe,' he commented. Right there and then, I knew Eamonn would invite the twins to take to the three-in-one sports option. Five years later, Chloe won para-triathlon silver at the Commonwealth Games.

Chloe recalls, 'We were over at the rowing tests. Eamonn was standing behind us. He caught up with us later and said rowing uses similar muscles to triathlon. He invited us to a para-triathlon training day in Belfast the following month. We exchanged contact details, and that's where it all started.'

Para-triathlon is the adapted version of triathlon for athletes with physical disabilities. The sport is governed by World Triathlon. Distances vary, depending on the competition level. The Paralympic programme consists of a 750m swim, 20km cycle and 5km run.

B1, B2 and B3 athletes may compete in para-triathlon. Classes are combined for medal and ranking purposes. However, B1 athletes are allocated extra time – they start a few minutes before the others – to compensate for the extra time they might need in the transition phases.

Chloe and Judith's mum identified their albinism shortly after birth. As Chloe says, 'We've always had it, so we've not known any different.'

While always interested in the great outdoors, especially athletics, it wasn't until Chloe's teenage years that she developed a keener interest. 'I started karate and hiking as part of the Duke of Edinburgh's Award scheme.' The Duke's Scheme was introduced in 1956 by the late Prince Philip to build youth development skills and promote sport and leisure activities.

'Later, at Coleraine University, I started to take sport seriously,' recalls Chloe. 'I tried out and was accepted into the college women's rugby team. I never mentioned my sight to them, and it was never an issue. It was close physical contact. When you pass, you shout to whom you are passing to. When you want the ball, you shout also. So, it's obvious where the ball is. It's so easy to keep track as players converge on the tackles. It was an easy sport to fumble my way through in terms of my eyesight.'

Chloe also took up rowing at college and trained with the Irish para-rowing squad. At the Paralympic Expo seven years ago, she was minded to trying competition in other sports, and then came Eamonn.

Eamonn Tilley from Dublin's Ringsend was a talented young runner. The Liffey Valley AC athlete, coached by the eminent Nick Davis, ran for Dublin in national inter-county cross-country and competed for Ireland in mountain running. He also represented Ireland at triathlon.

'As a teen, I loved running, but triathlon was all-consuming,' says Eamonn. 'From competing, I progressed to coaching triathlon. From grassroots in the 80s to high performance and ultimately to being a para-triathlon technical director. I had responsibility for para-triathlon, which was new twelve years ago.'

When Eamonn saw the late Michael Delaney compete in the first World Triathlon Para-triathlon Series Finals in London in 2013, his head was turned. Excited, he returned home and engaged with all key players. As Eamonn puts it, 'We grew b/vi para-triathlon with the team – Triathlon Ireland, Paralympics Ireland, Vision Sports Ireland, coaches, guides, volunteers and other specialists in the field. The individual support came from Paul Strange, Philip Manuel, Johanne Rock, John Barrie and Shane Kenny. Guides included Dave Tilley, Stephen Teeling Lynch, Bryan McCrystal and Sean Husband, to name just a few. I must thank Shane Califf at Sport Ireland for steering us towards Government Dormant Accounts for funding.'

The competition breakthrough came when Catherine Walsh and Fran Meehan – London 2012 co-medallists – came out of retirement and chose para-triathlon. Eamonn says, 'The girls knew high performance. They were ace cyclists and runners, so all I had to do was get them to swim. We had less than two years, and we managed to get our 750m time down from twenty minutes to sub-fifteen minutes, phenomenal!

'Catherine now passes on the para high-performance women's mantle to the MacCombe twins.'

Chloe MacCombe enjoyed the monthly training sessions with Eamonn but says when it comes to competition it can be tricky. 'I started out as a poor swimmer, but my guide was strong in the water. I could run, but she couldn't. Then, there was sourcing a tandem as well as finding more guides. At the beginning, we would have taken any guide, any tandem.'

In time, Eamonn tracked down guide Catherine Sands from Newry. 'I don't know how Eamonn did it,' says Chloe. 'Every available weekend, Catherine and I meet up. I take the bus from Derry to Newry, an eight-hour round trip, and we train for several hours together.'

In between the specialist training with Catherine, Chloe joins Judith for local gym sessions as well as running – unguided where they are familiar with the territory – and tandem cycling with the guide support within the community.

As members of the TI para squad, Chloe and Judith compete in races in Ireland and further afield. Chloe has represented her country in the UK, Spain, Portugal and Abu Dhabi.

Chloe's career highlight was at the 2022 Commonwealth Games in Birmingham. 'Catherine and I had never raced with a large paying audience. We were confident we could medal, maybe a third place, but as the race progressed, we felt stronger and moved up to second. Silver! We were delighted!'

Lady Mary Peters – Northern Ireland's Olympic gold medallist from Munich '72 – is a most distinguished fan and supporter of Chloe and Judith. 'They're called the Tandem Twins,' Mary recently told *The Irish Times*. 'They're twenty-five years old, and I am mesmerised by them.'

'They live on a farm near Londonderry. They go to the city to do their training in the morning, and then they work on the farm in the afternoon.' You're somebody when you get the gold stamp from the legendary Mary Peters.

Eamonn Tilley has now moved on from TI and thanks Matt McCarron and Chris Kitchen and all staff and athletes who worked with him to build para-triathlons in Ireland.

He recommends triathlons for all, all ages, all abilities. There's a distance, a time for all levels.

Eamonn concludes, 'Meeting and coaching people with disabilities has changed my life. Like many athletes, I was inclined to self-focus but now I think team. As a coach, I learned to listen and share ideas. I had no understanding of visual impairment until twelve years ago. I'm learning, and I especially find the experience of guiding to be the true bonus.

'Every coach needs to relate to disability sport. You don't truly know how to coach until you work with a person with a disability. People with a disability can tell you much more than you think you know.'

43. Love is all around

Vi tennis with manager Liam O'Donohoe (Wexford) and player Babs Weiberg (Louth/Germany).

As a teenager, I would hop over the Great Wall of Crumlin into the Guinness Iveagh grounds to watch the girls play tennis. On a few occasions, I got the 'c'mon for a game'. Sadly, I couldn't see the fast balls, so no love, no deuce, and not even a juice afterwards.

During the 1980s, when explaining b/vi sports to the media and at conferences, I always dismissed tennis as a no-go.

Then, twelve years ago, Metro Sports in London mentioned Vision Sports in their vi tennis Facebook posts. We explored the game at our 2014/15 Mayfests with mixed success. My then fellow Vision Sports board member Caroline Sweeney sourced and paid for the expensive specialist soft-sound tennis balls.

As the balls quickly deflated, so did our interest until an incredible force of human nature, Liam O'Donohoe, began hounding us with emails, messages and phone calls.

At the time, Liam said, 'We'll have 100 b/vi players in a year, Joe.' My reply was, 'We'll be lucky to muster up two dozen players, Liam!'

Liam was right. We went on to compete in five world championships to date, hosting the 2018 Blind Tennis World Championships in Liam's beloved Shankill Tennis Club.

Vi tennis is played indoors on a standard court using a junior racket and an adapted sponge ball that makes a noise when it bounces. Balls are usually high-viz yellow, but this may vary. Standard tennis rules apply with just a few modifications: if you're totally blind, you're allowed three bounces. Those with partial sight are allowed two. Sighted players are allowed only one bounce. In terms of eyesight classifications, there are five categories from B1 to B5.

Wexford's Liam O'Donohoe is steeped in tennis. His grandad, James Mythen, with his partner Bertha Irvine, founded the Swastika Tennis Club in Liverpool (before swastika became a dirty word). Liam spent his eight-week summer breaks in his family's holiday caravan in Rosslare. From dawn to dusk, he was out on the homemade tennis court with the O'Halloran sisters – Lesley and the late Joanne – who both went on to represent Ireland in the prestigious Fed Cup (now known as the Billy Jean King Cup).

In 2015 Liam took on a new role within Tennis Ireland as lead at Enjoy Tennis. The Enjoy Tennis programme is for players with a disability who can learn and enjoy playing tennis in mainstream clubs around Ireland.

Liam recalls the moment in 2015 when he heard of vi tennis. 'With my colleague Peter Farrell, I travelled to London to meet the Lawn Tennis Association, as they had been catering for disability tennis for thirty years or so. At the end of the meeting, vi tennis was mentioned. I knew nothing about it. By coincidence, Metro Club for b/vi people were hosting their monthly tennis coaching in Islington that evening. I had ninety minutes to spare before flying home, so I hopped over. Within minutes, I was on the court with b/vi players. They were having so much fun. I got permission to video-record, took it back to Ireland, and that's where it began.

'Sport Ireland, through Una May, who has since become its CEO, brought Vision Sports Ireland and Tennis Ireland together and encouraged us to avail of funding from the government's Dormant Account Fund.

'We launched vi tennis at Vision Sports Mayfest 2016. We brought Amanda Green and Odette Batterell across from Metro Sports London to guide us. I did a presentation at Mayfest Talkfest the day before at ChildVision in Drumcondra. It turned into great fun as I batted some softballs in the air. They hit the indoor hall rafters and bounced in all directions, hitting some on their heads.

'On the day itself, President Michael D. Higgins came along to launch Mayfest. With his wife, Sabina, he came over to us and asked could they see the game being played. As we were just starting out, we had no players, but I got the Metro girls out on the court, and it was brilliant.'

Twelve months later, Liam had a squad of dozens of b/vi players and led a team to the Blind Tennis World Championships in Spain.

So, what prompted Liam to bring the 2018 World Championships to Dublin?

'Well, I was always an ambitious player. I was chatting with the German international Chris Kaplan and Amanda (Metro), and they were unsure where the championships could be held. I told them we could do that, not realising what I was getting everybody into. With a huge volunteer effort, we pulled it off in style. Eighteen countries joined us. Both Wally Roode and the late Brian Lenihan medalled while Ireland came third in the medals table.'

Alex Whelan, the blind football manager, recalls, 'Liam invited me to become Ireland tennis team manager, a huge honour for me. The tournament was just brilliant. The totally blind players blew me away. I remember watching two of the top players from Mexico and Japan, playing out a six-rally. Just amazing.'

Liam O'Donohoe says the magic moment came at the closing ceremony. 'Quite spontaneously, the Irish team started singing "Ireland's Call." Well, Holy God, to this day, the hairs still stand up every time I recall that moment. I can feel it right now.'

The world championships generated huge media interest, which included RTÉ *Six One News* and later slots on RTÉ TV's *Nationwide* and *Winning Streak.*

Babs Weiberg was one of the many who signed up to vi tennis after the championships.

'In October 2018 I joined the coaching sessions (supported by Louth Local Sports Partnerships with Vision Sports Ireland and Enjoy Tennis). Three months later, I was at the nationals at Shankill and was awarded "Player of the Tournament". Then Liam called to say that I was going to Spain to represent Ireland at the world championships. I asked him if he was on the Guinness!'

Babs adds, 'Given the chance, I'd play five days a week, nine to five. I spend every spare cent I have on tennis. When my friend calls me for a coffee, I say, please come over to my house. I need the price of the coffee for my tennis.'

If you meet Babs on the streets of her adopted hometown of Dundalk, she'll pop a soft-sound tennis ball out of her pocket and persuade you to play the game. She carries that ball everywhere.

A decade after pioneering Enjoy Tennis in Ireland, Liam O'Donohoe tells us the winning secret: 'Simply, the smiles on every player's face.'

44. Marguerite time

Vi tennis player Marguerite Quinn (Limerick).

Marguerite Quinn is an extraordinary woman. I first met her at Mayfest '23. The story she told simply blew me away. Within days I made that call, recorded our chat, and here's what she told me about the day that changed her life ...

Marguerite opens by saying, 'I asked my doctor how I could quickly explain to people what happened to me on that Sunday morning, and this is the sentence she gave me: "I had a catastrophic bleed, not conducive to life."

'This sentence has become a mantra to me on days when I've lost motivation or on days when I'm not as grateful for all that I have in my life: great family, friends, neighbours and support staff.

'As my children and my husband prepared to leave the hospital that evening, they were told I won't wake up again.'

Five years later, Marguerite Quinn (fifty-eight) from Mungret, Co. Limerick, represented Ireland in a tennis tournament in Poland, placing third. A lifelong sport lover - camogie player, coach and administrator - Marguerite fought her way back from that close encounter through sport.

As Ireland braced itself for Storm Ophelia in October 2017, Marguerite was watching her daughter play camogie, unaware her own personal hurricane was about to hit.

'I felt a little under the weather, but I had phone calls to make. As principal of St Nessan's National School in Mungret, I needed to consult with the other local principals to determine when and if we would close due to Ophelia.'

While on the phone, Marguerite was having an aneurysm – an outward bulging caused by a weak spot on a blood vessel wall. She froze and lost consciousness. Twelve hours later, the medics said it was touch and go. Twelve months later, Marguerite was wheeled out of hospital.

'The following day, I was taken to Cork University Hospital, where the doctors waited at least a week before deciding to undertake the craniotomy procedure to clip my brain aneurysm. After a week and a half of recovery in Cork, I was brought home to Limerick, where I was now out of the induced coma. Slowly, I began to react and mumble, I had to work my way towards getting out of bed.

'A few weeks out of the coma, I felt there was something wrong with my eyes. They told me I was fine. I persisted, and they did a scan and found there had been a bleed at the back of the eye. They also found blood had got into the optic nerve. The blood had no release cavity, it was a catastrophic bleed.'

Marguerite has now no peripheral vision but some central vision, with a sport classification of B3.

The cause of the aneurysm? 'Jury out, as we will never know why the aneurysm burst on that particular day.'

Marguerite was back walking for short distances, using a wheelchair for more demanding journeys. She transferred from University Hospital Limerick to the National Rehabilitation Hospital in Dun Laoghaire in the summer of 2018.

Once on her feet, she was ready to challenge the world, get back to teaching, travel and sport. However, she may have hit the invisible barrier of what some Americans call 'attitudinal', a lesser-known but common issue for people with disabilities.

'I think people got caught in chapter three where they felt I was lucky to be alive. They got stuck on that line. I'm not complaining as everyone was so good and supported me. But I needed to get back to living.'

Marguerite, like so many with a variety of disabilities, conditions and life-fulfilling wishes, would have preferred if people trusted her and her knowledge of herself, and asked her where she wanted to go in chapters four, five, six …

To write the next chapters in sport, Marguerite began her research. 'I knew it couldn't be contact sport. I thought about coaching, but you need eyes in the back of your head for that. I knew golf was out there, but knew my balance wasn't right then due to the illness. So, I turned to the gym to rebuild strength, fitness and balance. I sorted my nutrition. I self-coached, being motivated to prove to people, I could be as good as anyone else, not better, just as good.

'In late 2019 I found a vi tennis taster day in Killaloe on the Vision Sports Ireland Facebook page. I made the call and joined coach Wesley O'Brien.

'Wesley stood behind me as I played and spoke. "Marguerite, you're telling me lies," he said. "No, I'm not, I am fifty-seven." "I'm not talking about your age," said Wesley, "I'm talking about you saying you never played tennis before. You couldn't have a backhand and forehand like that without having previously played." I told him he didn't ask me the right question; I was a camogie player.'

Marguerite had now found her perfect sport. With Wesley, she trained regularly, and, once Covid eased, she was capped for Ireland at the World VI Tennis Championships in Birmingham

'23. Following a successful week of tennis, Marguerite was ranked fourth in the world in her B3 category. She continues her travels with tennis and strives for further achievements to share with her band of supporters.

'Tennis is my focus, my release. On the court, I feel in control. In my life, a lot of the time, I don't feel in control. By control, I mean just knowing what I wanted and knowing how to get it correct and knowing how to get there. In my teaching career, I was brilliant at controlling.

'If I'm trying to learn a new tennis shot, slice or serve, I know what I must do. Now, it's different in that I do have to go step one, step two, step three. I must be methodical, as I must retrain my brain. Sometimes the clear focus can take away the pressure of something else going on in my life.

'The other complication is I have my old tricky brain fighting my new brain. The tricky brain must be controlled.'

Vi tennis ensures Marguerite makes it game, set and match for the new brain.

45. **The boat that I row**

Water sports with Shane Ryan (Limerick), Michael Lavin (Roscommon), Hilary Devlin (Dublin) and Rahim Nazarali (Dublin/Kenya), including kayaking, rowing, sailing and water-skiing.

Shane Ryan from Ballybricken in Co. Limerick is the first blind person to row the Atlantic from Europe to South America.

While we endured global lockdown, Shane escaped and joined his five-member crew and set out on an epic voyage beginning at the beautiful marina in Lagos, Portugal. He then tripped by Lanzarote and tipped by the North African coastline, including Morocco, before heading west towards French Guyana, off the shores of South America.

The voyage started with a sprint but ended with them rowing home backwards because a shark took their rudder for dinner. They endured famines and feasts. They feared being refused South American entry due to Covid, but that was sorted just two days before they made port.

Shane was born with Bardet-Biedl syndrome (BBS), a rare condition that caused his vision to deteriorate from his early teens. He now has 5 per cent vision.

He raised funds as part of his Atlantic crossing for Vision Sports Ireland: 'They helped me personally in the past. Without their services, I would not have been introduced to the sport of rowing many years ago. This ultimately led to my partaking in the London Paralympic Games in 2012 alongside another vision-impaired rower, Sarah Caffrey.'

When not in the water, Shane sets world indoor rowing records on his Concept2 rowing machine. He has set world records for longest distance in thirty minutes and sixty minutes. He also holds the number-one spot for the fastest time over 10km and the half marathon.

Indoor or outdoor rowing is a natural sport for b/vi people. In 1930s London, the rowing competitions for b/vi ladies on the Thames at Putney drew the crowds. There was an inter-rivalry between the newly formed London Blind Sports Club and Swiss Cottage School for Blind Girls.

B/vi rowers may seek qualification for para-rowing at the Paralympic Games. They may compete at PR3 coxed 4s. This category includes rowers with residual function in the legs as well as athletes with vision impairment.

Michael Lavin, who has served multiple years as League chair and secretary, loved the sailing experience. He comments: 'In 1981, the International Year of Disabled Persons, two prestigious yacht clubs, the Royal St George and the National in Dun Laoghaire, introduced us to Glenans, a French sail training club, which had a Dublin base. We learned so much about sailing, and I spent a fortnight developing skills in Bere Island. My wife Theresa stayed in Baltimore with Glenans for a similar period.'

As Michael and crew raised the mast, Hilary Devlin took to the waters and went wild with her sister, Caroline Casey. Hilary and Caroline have low vision due to albinism.

When I recently called her for a chat, she was on her own boat in Mayo.

'Dad taught us to sail when we were six or seven,' recalls Hilary. 'We did all the training courses as children and sailed across Ireland. Looking back, if I hadn't sailed, I would have had a sedentary childhood, as most of my mainstream schooling centred around unsuitable high-contact, fast-ball sports.

'Sailing is a pleasure. When you can't drive, it's just great to get on the water, steer the boat and harness the wind to take you where you want to go. Two days ago, I was out on the boat with my son Mathew (eight). I told him I could capsize today, but he wasn't to worry. I capsized for the first time in twenty-five years, but I could right the boat. Scary for us, but the adrenaline, that's something else.'

Kayaking is another water sport where you can take quite a tumble. While in London training to be a physiotherapist thirty-five years ago, Paralympic medallist Fintan O'Donnell took the plunge.

'I joined a local kayaking club. We went whitewater kayaking around the UK and down into the south-east of France. I trained as a river leader, but rather than lead groups, I usually operated as the safety lead, bringing up the rear. I had friends who accepted I could travel with them closer than would be normal. I was lucky to meet people who were happy to facilitate my needs and be my guides, although I may not follow them faithfully.'

Water-ski weekends at Carrig Wake in Cork were the hottest ticket in town from 1997 to pre-Covid. I fondly remember calls from Sarah McLoughlin at the Vision Sports Ireland office. 'Joe, the water-ski weekend tickets sold out in ten minutes. What are we going to do?' Sarah would then ring our judo star Rahim Nazarali, and, somehow, between the two of them, the waters parted, and they performed a miracle. Another weekend, more tickets to issue.

'I began travelling to Carrig Wake in 2003 and attended most years thereafter,' recalls Rahim. 'I progressed from skiing with a buddy to going on my own. The guys would blow a whistle and indicate a left or right turn with the boat. I then progressed from the skis to the wakeboard, which is like a surfboard on the water. I learned how to go backward and forward pushing. It's a skill that requires agility and balance.'

Ireland has a world champion b/vi water skier in Janet Gray from Co. Down. Now retired from the sport, Janet won three World titles two decades ago.

Skiing is believing.

46. **Take it to the limit**

Zero limits at Mondello with Aaron Mullaniff, CEO, Vision Sports Ireland, and Sara McFadden (Mayo). B/vi people drive dual-controlled cars.

'If there was a way of holding up a mirror to an event that has exceeded our wildest expectations, it has to be Zero Limits.'

I'm chatting with Aaron Mullaniff, CEO of Vision Sports Ireland and Vision Ireland's chief services officer. He's excited about a new annual event, where b/vi participants drive dual-controlled cars at Dublin's Mondello Park racetrack. Later, they take the passenger seat and race with Ireland's top rally drivers taking the controls.

Zero Limits is a collaboration between Vision Sports Ireland and Motor Sport Ireland. 'It's an ocean of emotion to witness b/vi people experience driving for the first time or the first time in years,' says Aaron. 'It is very emotional. We started out with fifty participants in 2021. In 2023, we had 120 and could have sold that event out ten times over.

'Zero Limits evolved from an internal Vision Ireland thought process as to how we could challenge perceptions of blindness and vision impairment in a positive light. I was looking for a conduit that could tick many boxes: inclusion, collaboration, partnership, sustainability and education, where the perceived impossible could be made possible. Eventually, I looked at the most unlikely sport in the world: motorsport. Soon, Zero Limits was born.

'I probably never had an easier task in getting backing from a corporate. I approached Windsor Motors, and they immediately said yes. Sport Ireland had no hesitation in endorsing and later supporting the event. That support included Sport Ireland CEO Una May who announced to the crowd this year that Zero Limits is her favourite event to attend ' With cheques in hand, the chequered flag at Mondello was raised.

Aaron Mullaniff is from the GAA stronghold of Edenderry, Co. Offaly, where he attended St Mary's primary and secondary schools. He was a keen footballer and played underage for Offaly before moving to soccer with various Dublin clubs, including Shelbourne. He initially qualified with a degree in leisure management with a follow-up master's in health services management from Trinity and another master's in business leadership & management practice from UCD.

He first ventured into physio and physical training with Rhode GAA, but 'rubbing down twenty hairy men on a Friday night wasn't for me'.

He stepped into sports development with the Mullingar Youth Development Programme, 'Keeping young fellas out of trouble where sporting chance was the distraction,' before working with Westmeath Local Sports Partnership. Stints working and studying in the USA and Australia followed before he joined Vision Ireland as their rehabilitation co-ordinator.

'It was there I discovered Vision Sports. We were short of sports equipment, so they helped me get a few exercise bikes through grant aid. B/vi people were having difficulties accessing conventional facilities and exercise. I remember developing their first personalised programmes, focusing on balance and spatial awareness, bringing science and physio to the job.'

A few years later, in 2015, I met Aaron for the first time. He hasn't been the same since. Aaron is a strategy and ideas man par excellence who strongly supports the belief that almost everything is possible. 'Yes, if you can drive a car for the first time after blindness or vision impairment, you can try anything.'

He singles out b/vi rally navigator Sara McFadden. 'She is simply brilliant. The event would not be possible without her and her incredible network: her mum and dad, the rally family of volunteers, and our partners, Motor Sport Ireland.'

Sara McFadden recalls steering Zero Limits onto the road. 'We had a great person in Aaron driving us on. Putting together Zero Limits was enormous. We set out to organise an event like no other with a highly dedicated but small Vision Sports crew.

'Behind the scenes, it was very stressful. We had huge challenges in areas like risk management. I had the rallying and motorsport contacts; I knew them personally, and they all dropped everything to volunteer. It turned into a phenomenal event, better than anything on offer internationally.'

Sara has friends in high places, including world-famous rally champion and 1960s icon the late Rosemary Smith, who attended Zero Limits in 2021 and 2022.

'I've been to Mondello many times over the years,' said Rosemary Smith. 'But the enthusiasm and energy at Vision Sports' Zero Limits track day was like nothing else I've experienced here before. The delight on the faces of the participants after the morning driving experience, followed by the excitement of getting into a rally car, was so special. It was an honour to get behind the wheel of the Renault Twingo and share this experience with them. I am an advocate for changing perceptions, chasing new experiences, and doing what you love.'

Sara McFadden, who has 10 per cent vision, also had the opportunity to drive at Mondello. 'Coming from a rallying family, I knew I could never drive on an open road. Zero Limits gave me the opportunity to drive and recover from a skid. When I got out of the car the first time, all I could scream to friends and family was, "Did you see my driving skills?" It's so emotional and so many people – our b/vi drivers, their co-drivers, our high-speed rally drivers, spectators – just cried our eyes out with excitement.

'My cousin Sarah was concerned about one b/vi participant who had just finished a lap and was bawling crying. Sarah asked if she was okay. The participant nodded and asked for a hug. Sarah, who was head to toe in racing and Covid safety gear, said "YES, OF COURSE!" They hugged, and the participant simply said, "I never thought I could experience this. I never thought I would experience this." I bumped into the participant moments later, and she said, "Now I understand why you do this, Sara."'

As for the reaction of the rallying and motorsport community: 'A top international rally driver who stepped back from the sport to do charity track days congratulated me. He then told me Zero Limits was the best event he had ever participated in. When he saw me blush, he stepped back and added it was almost as good as an international meet he was involved in.

'Another driver told me at our first event that he was sorry he only brought one rally car along. He'd bring four next time, and he did.

'We had a guy who drove a truck and car from London to be with us on day one. By day two, his car had blown up. It cost him a massive five-figure sum to repair. He was due to but unable to race the following weekend. He simply smiled and said he'd be back next year. He got so much out of living and loving it all.

Sara adds, 'When everyone went home after our first year, and a few of us were left behind cleaning up, a friend came over and ordered me to get my helmet on. I did, I hopped into his rally car, and we sped off around the track. We had such fun and when we finished, I was smiling from ear to ear. My normal weekend rally navigating is in a competitive sport with no time for fun.'

A lap of honour for Sara in a world of zero limits.

47. Waterfront

Swimmer Róisín Ní Riain (Limerick).

'I was thrilled. I couldn't believe it. I didn't know as I couldn't see the [results] board. It was when I got out of the pool that somebody told me I had won.'

At eighteen years of age, Róisín Ní Riain from Drombanna, Co. Limerick, had just completed the race of her life to take gold in the 100m backstroke at the IPC World Para Swimming Championships. It was 3 August 2023 in Paris as Róisín became the first Irish b/vi swimmer to win a world title.

Róisín was born with coloboma, which impacts her visual field and acuity, leaving her with less than 10 per cent sight.

She took her first dip into swimming at age four. 'I loved it instantly,' Róisín says. 'I've always been a water child and knew from the start it was my sport. I began competing at nine or ten after joining my local Limerick Swimming Club. I progressed through the levels – schools, regionals, community games, nationals – then in the middle of Covid, I began in para-swimming and competed internationally.'

Róisín's route to para-sport proved quite the adventure as she sought international sight classification in Italy. 'The trip was planned for February 2020. The night before we were due to depart, Italy went into Covid lockdown. Eventually, I travelled a year later and got my classifications. In competition, I achieved the minimum qualification for the Paralympics. Success, I got the job done.

'Then we returned to Dublin Airport and had to quarantine.'

For a highly active athlete, how did she cope with ten days in isolation, 175km from her Limerick home? 'Interesting, but not too bad,' says Róisín. 'At the time, national swimming championships were taking place. Once I completed all Covid tests and took the necessary precautions, allowances were made to enable me to compete in the final days of Olympic and Paralympic swim trials. I then completed quarantine, which was isolating and not the news you want to hear, but it did give me time to rest, recover and prepare for the competitions ahead.'

A month later, Róisín returned to Dublin Airport Arrivals, but this time, they did not lock her up. Instead, it was anything to declare as she produced a glittering bronze medal. She finished third in the 100m backstroke at the IPC European Para-Swimming Championships in Madeira, her first major para-sport medal.

By summer's end, she was at the Tokyo Paralympic Games as the youngest member of the Irish team. 'Not many expectations beyond giving it my all in every race, taking in the experience.

'I was very happy over there. I swam six races, reaching the finals in five with PBs along the way.'

In June 2022 Róisín returned to Madeira and won double bronze at the IPC World Para Swimming Championships in the 100m backstroke and breaststroke. After completing her Leaving Cert, our Limerick teenager re-focused to become the gold star of the 2023 IPC Worlds in Paris. While in Paris she also won silver at 100m butterfly.

Award nominations followed, including both the 2023 RTÉ Sports Person of the Year and the 2023 Young Sports Person of the Year.

In April 2024, at the IPC European Para Swimming Championships, in Madeira once more, Róisín won a massive five medals to double her overall haul to date to ten. She won gold at both 100m breast stroke and backstroke; double silver at the 100m butterfly and 200m individual medley as well as bronze at 400m freestyle.

Achieving her pot of gold, silver and bronze was no easy action for Róisín and involved a decade of build-up culminating in dawn-to-dusk training. 'I'm studying to be a science teacher at the University of Limerick (UL), and my accommodation is beside the pool. I get up at 5.45 each morning, and I'm at the pool by six. The training session begins at 6.30 and finishes at 8.30 or nine, depending on the type of session. Back then at four for another two to three hours, which may include gym work. After six days of training, I usually rest on Sunday.'

For the Paralympic sport of swimming, there are separate categories for B1 (S11), B2 (S12) and B3 (S13). Róisín competes at S13. Like many swimmers in her category, she must overcome the barriers of accurately identifying turning and finish points. Unlike many swimmers with low or no vision, she does not avail of a tapper to indicate turn and finish points.

When I asked Róisín about the key to her success, she beamed. 'Mum and Dad must get the first shout-out. They woke me up every morning for eight years to bring me to training. They brought me to all the competitions and got my food ready. We're a family of six, and we're all swimmers. I'm the oldest, with three sisters. Sorcha and Sadhbh are twins, while Meadhbh is the youngest.

'John Szaranek, who came to Limerick Swimming Club around 2019, is my coach. I have a great training group here at UL who inspire me every day. Likewise, I have my Paralympics Ireland training group and their support staff. I wouldn't be where I am without them.'

In her short international career to date, Róisín Ní Riain has made quite the splash. She's only just begun.

48. Brand-new key

Release from Covid-19 lockdown with Aaron Mullaniff and Pádraig Healy, National Sports Development Manager, Vision Sports Ireland.

We roared into the 20s as Vision Sports Ireland successfully merged with Vision Ireland. Then came Covid-19, the lockdowns and postponements of key events, including our Mayfest and, further afield, Tokyo 2020.

Aaron Mullaniff recalls: 'Just two weeks after our merge launch – with Dean Rock, Darragh Maloney and Jason Smyth – the Taoiseach announced lockdown. All my ideas and strategies went out the window. We knew immediately blind and vi people would be disproportionately affected as so many depended on guides to get outside.'

For my own contribution, I churned out weekly, rather than monthly, editions of *Vision Sports News*, which included uplifting stories and tips on how to beat the pandemic. I begged, stole and borrowed lots of adapted home-exercise routines. I had been editing newsletters since we began five decades ago, including the immensely successful *Sportslink* bi-monthly bulletin with colleagues the late Sean Hackett, Mary Keena and Anne and Tony Lyster.

Our ideas man, Aaron, produced an intriguing initiative. 'Eureka, the Epiphany, most blind people have a long cane, which we could use as a social-distancing tool.'

The solution allowed the blind runner/walker to take one end of an extended long cane, and their guide could lead with the other end while physically distancing 2 metres apart. With parkrun Ireland volunteers, the initiative got the thumbs up from many b/vi people, some even saying they preferred it to the standard guide wrist-to-wrist tether format.

Aaron sums it up. 'This solution was so popular that it may have been our best recruitment drive. To think it was in the middle of a pandemic.'

I developed a solution, which Aaron and his colleague Kristina Millar branded as 'Pass-Sport'. The b/vi sportsperson registered their designated guide/pilot with Vision Sports Ireland, and, subject to terms and conditions, they could travel together to and from a sports/leisure facility; walk, run, swim, or other similar exercise activity, play golf, tennis, football, or tandem cycle.

Pass-Sport received special praise from the government Return to Sport Committee, which sanctioned the nationwide initiative.

By November 2020 it seemed everyone was doing Zoom games, quizzes and exercise classes. With the Vision Sport team, I developed Nice2MetreYou, another Aaron Mullaniff brand name. Our team had fireside chats with friends, including Paralympians Jason Smyth, Katie-George Dunlevy and Italian rugby international Ian McKinley.

Despite all the initiatives, lockdowns were having a greater impact on b/vi people than on the population in general. To monitor, Vision Sports Ireland conducted snapshot member surveys. In January 2021, 84 per cent of members said Covid restrictions were majorly impacting engagement in physical activity, down from 90 per cent in May 2020. On the other hand, those reporting a considerable negative impact on their mental health increased from 50 per cent in May 2020 to 55 per cent eight months later. Also, in January 2021, 81 per cent indicated they were participating in less exercise per week than pre-lockdown in January 2020.

Then Mr Fixit arrived. Pádraig Healy came on board as National Sports Development Manager and introduced multiple home-grown exercise programmes specifically tailored to the needs of b/vi people. With Pádraig, we identified funds to support our members to purchase the required equipment to exercise at home. Four years later, the Vision Sports Ireland home exercises series continues to grow and is very popular with members.

I recently caught up with Pádraig at the Granville Hotel on Meagher's Quay in Waterford, home to our great friends, the Cusack family.

Pádraig Healy from Dungarvan in Waterford was born into athletics. His dad was an underage champion with Middleton AC, while his mum preferred to officiate at all levels, including the 2002 IAAF World Cross-Country Championships at Leopardstown, Dublin.

Pádraig loved sport and competed successfully in football, hurling, soccer, swimming and cycling. In athletics, he was a team member of winning All-Ireland intermediate and senior cross-country teams. On the track at college, Pádraig captained CIT (now MTU in Cork). Inter-varsity rivalry can't have been too bad, as Pádraig later married the UCC club captain Tara.

Having an uncle with an intellectual disability, some gentle persuasion from his late mother along with a college work placement with Carriglea Cairde Services for residents with intellectual disability introduced Pádraig to a whole new world, which he grew to love.

Later, armed with his Business in Recreation and Leisure Management degree, he became the Sports Inclusion Disability Officer (SIDO) with Local Sports Partnerships in Cork and Kildare. His annual Sports Ability Days became the model for sports partnerships nationwide.

SIDOs nationwide play a very welcome and critical role in developing and promoting sport for people with disabilities.

Having honed his skills at SIDO, Pádraig couldn't resist taking on the challenge of managing the small volunteer-led Vision Sports Ireland. 'Times were changing with sports, and it was increasingly difficult for voluntary-led organisations. It was a brand-new role for the organisation, exciting but also a little daunting.'

Pádraig, with Aaron Mullaniff, built the organisation from employing two part-timers to a staff of seven, including five working full-time.

'Vision Sports is always going to be a small governing body,' says Pádraig. 'A huge part of our role is to leverage the larger governing bodies to include our members in their activities.

'Building capacity in the community is key. Last year, we had over 200 people enrol in our ninety-minute online certified Vision Sports Awareness course. The course includes basic information on types of vision impairments, guiding, colour contrasting and much more. The aim is to support the community, volunteers, coaches, and teachers in providing a positive experience for our members in mainstream activities.

'We have developed a three-hour practical tandem pilot course with Cycling Ireland. In addition, we do a ninety-minute in-person guide running course with Athletics Ireland.

'We are also developing sport-specific resources in PDF format for coaches and volunteers. We have completed the b/

vi rugby resource and are progressing on football and athletics. We are also launching an intervention to support teachers in the education sector with an information pack and equipment.'

Now three years working with Vision Sports, has his perception of blindness and their sports requirements changed?

'There's a belief out there that most b/vi people have no sight. It's the opposite, with just 5 per cent with total blindness. However, while small in numbers, these members require the most support. This realisation has helped us focus on programmes for those with no sight.'

In 2023 Pádraig and his team, in association with Mason Hayes & Curran, introduced an Education Bursary. The bursary is aimed at supporting students who are b/vi to pursue their academic goals by providing financial assistance of up to €2,000 per annum for the duration of their undergraduate degree up to a maximum of €8,000.

In a fast-changing b/vi sports landscape, we are very fortunate to have Pádraig Healy to lead the way.

49. Here comes tomorrow

The next phase.

I'm no angel and have spiked, and been spiked, on and off the track.

The falls while training or racing can be an occupational hazard when you're b/vi. Thankfully, the only time I ended up in a hospital emergency department was when a dog bit me in the ass. The falls in sports administration are harder to take. You fall, stand up again. Thankfully, I can count these falls on one hand. Almost everyone I fell out with, I fell back in with again, and we remain good friends. Sports administration is tough. Add disability and multi-sport to the mix, and you're in real trouble,

Life's been good to me with many personal, occupational and sports highlights. On the sports field, I'm proud to be a Paralympian as well as being a Euro 5000m silver medallist. At the sports desk, I loved playing key roles in the hosting of the Dublin Euros of 1993 and developing Mayfest, joining friends and having turns at the wheel to steer Vision Sports Ireland to where it is now.

I'm a proud member of the community that built nationally organised b/vi sport and recreation activities in Ireland. In this book, we meet some, but there simply wasn't enough space to meet so many more warm, wonderful people. In a cast of thousands, there are so many more stars with incredible life stories just waiting to burst out.

I had a lucky escape three decades ago when I met disgraced swim coach George Gibney and verbally offered him the role of national b/vi coach. When I sought sanction from my board, two members shook their heads. Puzzled, I withdrew the request and told Gibney the appointment was postponed. Months later, George Gibney was accused of child sexual offences, faced court and left the country.

My most difficult yet rewarding admin experience was the 2018–20 Vision Sports Ireland/Vision Ireland merge. Like several others, I wrestled with my conscience on whether to merge or not. Vision Sports is a small governing body with a rich history and seriously superb achievements. It was volunteer-driven and, on occasions, struggled administratively and financially. On balance, I concluded that the Vision Sports Ireland/Vision Ireland merge was the way to go, and I successfully led and presented its case at our 2019 EGM.

I am thrilled with its success as it grows in reach and resources.

The merge was led by Chris White, Paul Ledwidge and Ruairi McGinley on the Vision Ireland side and by Fiona Cusack, Kevin Kelly, Rahim Nazarali and me at the Vision Sports Ireland end.

Aaron Mullaniff, chief bottlewasher at Vision Sports, says there's more work to be done but that for a long time, 'Vision Ireland has offered many services to its users. Now, we can further develop the core services of sport and participation, physical activity, and wellness across the country. This is my number-one priority.'

Des Kenny, the former NCBI CEO, believes, 'As b/vi people, we are best able to determine what we want and how we want to see structures.' Solid advice from a man who knows.

Many b/vi people note the progress in disability awareness that has developed over many decades. However, it is also said we may only be at the halfway line when it comes to education and understanding.

1996 Paralympic gold medallist Bridie Lynch says, 'Disability awareness, including sport and recreation, must be included in the primary school curriculum. This could include structured school visits by people with disabilities.'

Bridie believes everyone's a winner. 'The child who never encountered disability and the disabled pupil who may find a new dignity and learns that the sky is the limit with most things possible.'

Media awareness of disability here is lagging, but it has come a long way in the past five decades. In 1981, on returning from the Euro Championships in West Germany, I handed the results to a senior sports journalist. Not a word was printed. I asked a mutual friend to find out why. The answer: the journo believed we were not playing by the same rules as mainstream athletes and our times/distances were not being properly measured.

British-based Irish Paralympian Katie-George Dunlevy says, 'Huge media coverage kicked in in Britain during and after London 2012, and it has been growing ever since. Live TV coverage, particularly on Channel Four, extra programmes, news bulletins and interviews with British Paralympians on talk, game and reality TV shows. They are all celebrities known to everybody.' Except for Jason Smyth – following his victory on RTÉ's *Dancing with the Stars* in March 2024 – our Paralympians and their sports are little known in Ireland.

We are fortunate to have the RTÉ Sports Personality Awards, *Dancing with the Stars* and reporters attending the Paralympic

Games, but there may be a case for following the chimes of Big Ben and keeping up with the changing times.

Many in advocacy groupings in the disability sports and welfare sector are in awe of the Sport Ireland-promoted Women in Sport campaign. They feel a similar campaign for People with Disabilities in Sport could reap massive rewards. While such a campaign could be multi-pronged, the awareness element could include a prime-time TV series where people with a variety of disabilities – led by our sports stars – could bring viewers through a day in the life, including the good, the bad and the ugly. Such a series – entertaining but educational – could be supported by mainstream and social media.

Bridie Lynch would certainly back such a campaign as she is keen to emphasise that each disability is different and bunching all together is wrong. Wheelchair tennis and blind tennis are different sports, just as lawn tennis and table tennis are different.

Over the years, I have had many discussions with people about pan-disability administration, where one overarching authority takes care of all disabled sports. Some able-bodied administrators like the idea, and some do not. Absolutely NO disabled athlete has ever spoken in favour of the idea, so let's hope we never head down that road in Ireland.

Accepting disability can be an issue. Bridie Lynch points out, 'Disabled children and young adults may struggle to adapt to their disability. Jason Smyth, a teenage star athlete, was reluctant to be seen as a Paralympian. Jason cleared that hurdle, and now look at him. Jason has led the way for anyone with a disability to participate in mainstream and para-sports.'

The barriers around accessibility are often highlighted but not always acted on.

For Pádraig Healy, National Sports Development Manager at Vision Sports Ireland, there is one big challenge to overcome: 'Transport is a huge barrier for b/vi people, it's affecting our participation levels as we are constantly told members cannot get to activities. It's a particular problem in rural areas where the Free Travel Scheme is often of no value with non-availability of public transport.'

Pádraig advocates for a government Transport Allowance to enable b/vi people to avoid isolation and enable them to participate in sport and leisure activities.

When free travel was mentioned in the past, the answer was 'PASS'. Let's hope the government listen to Pádraig and doesn't pass.

Many b/vi sportspeople have accessibility issues with gym equipment. It is, therefore, very welcome that Peloton now uses Android Talkback while more exercise apps, which map onto gym equipment such as exercise bikes, are screen-reader compatible. Most smart wearables now have screen-reader capability. However, for the non-techies, simple things such as tactile markings and voice-over on core gym equipment would be beneficial. A lot done, but more to ensure accessibility is there for all.

International vi tennis player Babs Weiberg believes, 'No new sports facilities should be built without first consulting with b/vi people. Simple suggestions before the design stages are finished could make such facilities so accessible later.'

On overall organisation and governance, Pádraig Healy muses: 'Our ideal should be that Vision Sports Ireland will not exist someday. That every sport NGB is inclusive of all abilities.'

Notwithstanding the ideal, Pádraig agrees that for b/vi sportspeople, while mainstreaming is important, the benefits of meeting peers at events such as Mayfest, Zero Limits and Camp Abilities are clear. We will always wish to compete on a level footing against one another in many sports at all levels. The b/vi sports landscape has evolved at a rapid pace over recent decades, so the future is open.

It may be b/vi sport, baby, but not as we know it.

50. After the gold rush

Jason Smyth MBE.

On 29 March 2023, Jason Smyth MBE – undefeated champion of the Paralympic World – retired.

From 2005 to 2021, Jason won twenty-one Paralympic, World and European Gold medals. He is the current Paralympic World Record holder at T13 100m and 200m.

Jason won three Athletics Ireland national 100m titles and was the first-ever Paralympian to compete at the European Athletics Championships. He also represented Ireland at the World Athletics Championships as well as Northern Ireland at the Commonwealth Games. His 100m personal best time of 10.22 was .04 seconds outside the qualifying time for the 2012 Olympic Games.

Off track, Jason has been a habitual nominee for the RTÉ Sports Person of the Year. In December 2023 he received the supreme accolade when being inducted into the RTÉ Sports Hall of Fame. In early 2024 Jason won the nation over on RTÉ's *Dancing with the Stars*, where he was victorious, taking home the coveted glitterball.

While people with 0 per cent vision face the greatest challenges, how does Jason manage with 10 per cent sight? What impact does low vision have on his day-to-day living, his training, his racing? Recently, Jason and I got chatting, and I asked him to explain.

Joe: You began to lose sight at an early age?

Jason: Yep. Mum and Dad realised I would move closer to the TV, and when I was trying to look at them, I was looking past them. I was having to get closer to stuff at school. They brought me to an optician and then an eye specialist at the hospital.

At seven or eight, I can't remember exactly where or when I became aware that I had a sight problem. I do recall Mum crying at the time. I was too young to understand. My sight was fading, but what you see is normal to you, although not to someone else.

Joe: Your eye condition is Stargardt disease, the most common inherited single-gene retinal disease. It's progressive, can stabilise and usually affects children?

Jason: Yes. My grandad William had this condition, but it wasn't diagnosed until he was sixty.

Joe: So, what can you see?

Jason: The centre part of my eye is a blind spot. It's not black or white; it's invisible, like it doesn't exist. Outside that centre point, I have a full field of vision. Because of colour contrast, I can see everything around me, but I can't see detail: It's blurry.

Joe: Day to day, what can you see?

Jason: Take a large bus, for example. As the bus gets closer, I can probably see it, but I can never see the number or where it's going. If I'm at a stop with ten different buses, how do I know which bus is the one that I want to stop? Some bus stops have real-time displays, which may be too high to see. I can overcome this by taking a photo and zooming into the image. Recognising people is an issue. I can see people walking past me because I can see colour and movement, but I can never see a person's face to identify them. I can't see them looking at me to know if they're talking to me. I remember after London 2012, I walked past a friend of a friend who had tried to engage me, wave to me. He then told my friend I was ignorant and arrogant. Like many, my disability is invisible. They cannot see what I can and cannot see. It's so different to having a guide dog or a long cane.

Joe: You lose independence, too?

Jason: Yeah. Driving is the big one. It determines where I can and cannot live, and I must live near public transport links. Houses may, therefore, cost more. Once I make it to public transport, it may double the time I need to reach my destination. Training at the Sport Ireland facilities at Abbotstown is a disaster as I must take two trains and a taxi to get there. Some areas have no public transport at all, so I rely on others to drive me. When I trained in Florida, my coach drove me to training. Not being able to drive means more planning and lots of patience.

Joe: Back to your schooldays now. Did vision impact your choice of sport?

Jason: Not massively. I was naturally sporty and fast. As I got older, anything I lacked in not seeing, I made up for with my speed. I played all sports and loved soccer, and I still do. At grammar school, I played rugby, tennis and cricket. Okay, I could never reach my physical potential in some sports as the vision just wasn't there. The reality is some sports use small or high balls, which are too difficult to follow. In other sports, you can play to your strengths. Nowadays, I play football with my friends on a Monday evening. When the ball is around me, I'm in control. If I'm on the other side of the pitch and someone passes the ball from a distance, there's every chance I'll miss it entirely. So, I stay central, so those long passes only travel half the distance.

Joe: Athletics found you in your mid-teens.

Jason: I wasn't much bothered as I was more interested in football and other stuff. My teacher, Liz Maguire, who was into athletics, suggested I give it a try. I asked her to come back with the information, hoping she wouldn't, but she did. So, I had to keep up my end of the deal and went down to the local club. There, Stephen Maguire spotted me and invited me into his group. Stephen has been my coach for many years now.

Joe: You were soon an underage sprint champ?

Jason: It happened quickly. Within the first year of going to training, I had qualified for the U18 Commonwealth Games and was Irish Schools Champion.

Joe: What propelled you into para-sport?

Jason: Yeah, I knew nothing about the Paralympics and probably assumed the Paralympics and Special Olympics were the same. I attended training for a year and my coach, Stephen, wasn't aware of my sight problem. I never told him as I stuck behind people while training in a group. Then my dad said something to him. Maybe a couple of years later, Stephen mentioned that I may qualify for the Paralympics. Would I be interested?

I had a battle with myself. My perception of the Paralympics back then was that these were circles I wanted not to be seen in. I was trying to hide my lack of vision rather than stand up and shine a light on it. At school, I didn't want to be seen as different. If I became a Paralympian, I'd achieve the opposite, be seen as different and no longer be able to hide it.

I can't remember why I went for it, but it wasn't an easy decision. I knew I'd have a high world ranking. The decision to go with it probably lay with the opportunities and funding available. It took quite a few years before I felt comfortable and confident to talk about being a Paralympic athlete.

Joe: Your journey and ultimate success two decades ago have paved the way for thousands of disabled children and adults to accept and participate in disability sports.

Jason: Agree. It requires people to change it, change perception and I was one of those helping it happen. Another very important player here is Michael McKillop, who came up around at the same time. We had a lot of success.

Joe: And it all began at the Vision Sports Ireland 2005 Mayfest at ALSAA, beside Dublin Airport.

Jason: It's crazy, an amazing coincidence that Michael and I both began our Paralympic journey together on the same day, and we've been rooming together at para-athletics events for so many years.

Joe: Now that you're a Paralympian, how do you negotiate international travel, training, and competition?

Jason: If I've been there enough times, I can rely on memory rather than what I can see. Otherwise, I rely on other people. Many times, at airport departures, I have required assistance. But, again, when you get to the other end, I can't see signs, which could be in any language, so finding taxis or people with signs to pick you up is a problem. Then, when I arrive at an athletics track I haven't been to before, it's like, where's the check-in, the toilets, the changing rooms? It's constantly having to ask people things. When it comes to competition, I'll have someone with me, maybe my coach. During race warm-up, I must have someone with me, as athletes will be running up and down lanes, and I can't see where they are, whether they are slowing down or stopping.

Joe: Indoor competition is popular with Irish sprinters. How do you manage it?

Jason: There's another situation. I stopped doing indoors as the space was too small. Warm-ups where athletes run in every direction. I wasn't comfortable visually, while, again, athletes would not be aware of what I could and couldn't see.

Joe: Pre-race in other competitions, how do you manage in the dressing room?

Jason: Identifying competitors, eyeballing them, psyching them out. Well, it doesn't work with visually impaired people. I just focus on my race. The organisers take care of the details around guiding and reassuring you as to what you must do, where to go and where your lane is. Over time, experience builds confidence in preparation and following protocol. Possibly, in my early days, I might have been anxious about my surroundings and objects in my way that I may not see.

Joe: Any issues once you leave the changing rooms and enter the track?

Jason: A track is a track. I have been running up and down them across the world for eighteen years. There's a peace around being familiar with your environment. Before major competitions, there are usually a few days where you can walk the track, and hear the starter do a few starts. But that's for anybody, irrespective of sight. I think for visually impaired people, there is an element of you can't rely on your eyes. I like to be familiar with the situation before going into it, so I don't get surprises.

Joe: It's race day, you're about to go under starter's orders, what can you see around you?

Jason: I see blurry colours. I can't see the finish line. However, I can see the orange track and white lines to guide, but eventually, these lines become mushed up into one. Around the stadium, I can see colour differences. So, I may see green on the inside and assume this is the grass. On sunny days or on a poor track with lodged water, I'd wear dark glasses to remove glare.

Joe: On your marks, set, bang!

Jason: That brings me to London 2012 and the T13 100m heats. The black camera moved along with the athletes, but I could not see the detail to identify what it was. I thought there was somebody running right beside me. If I ran faster, it moved faster. So, it's just seeing the colour and making the wrong assumption.

Vision-impaired people struggle with dipping at the finish line. Sometimes you get it right. Lots of times, people get it wrong because you just can't anticipate and see the line as you approach. I went through a career without dipping.

Joe: Until your famous golden dip in Tokyo 2020.

Jason: Good time to get it right [laughing].

Joe: Post-race, any sight/navigation issues?

Jason: Athletes will never be allowed to wander around track and field during a live event, so I'd always be accompanied. Meeting media, well, they always identify themselves. Anti-doping? For obvious reasons, you can never be left on your own.

Joe: Post-race video analysis is common to all sports; how do you manage?

Jason: I can't visually see the details of video feedback. So, everything I do can be different, with solutions best suited to my needs. One thing my coach did well was interpret what was on video for me. I liked to feel what I was doing wrong. I knew what I was supposed to feel like, so then I could compare. My gauge was how I felt, not what I saw.

Joe: Finally, none of us are islands. We can only do what we do with supports?

Jason: I'm fortunate as I was winning medals, which was an advantage in getting support. In those early days, my parents were a massive support. Then there's Steven Maguire, my coach and mentor, who moved to Florida with me for four years so I could be with the best athletes in the world.

I look at a lot of other visually impaired and disabled people and realise the same access may not be there for them. I'll do what I can to help, but there will always be challenges to overcome.

There's no shortage of sporting legends in Ireland: Rachel Blackmore, Eamonn Coghlan, Ronnie Delaney, Kelly Harrington, Leona Maguire, Roy Keane, Sonia O'Sullivan, Jonnie Sexton, Katie Taylor and John Treacy.

All the above, and many more too, are worthy of sitting at the top table of sports here. But wait a minute, pull over a chair, boys and girls, for the champion of all champions, the man who was a world beater for his entire eighteen-year career. Sit down at the top of that table, Jason Smyth.

Acknowledgements

Many rules of popular modern sport were written in Great Britain and on the east coast of the USA in the mid-nineteenth century. Back then the concept of people with disabilities participating in sport could never have been considered. Adapted sport rules for b/vi people came into play in the second half of the twentieth century.

So, digging back over two centuries to find out what sport and leisure activities were played by b/vi people was always going to be difficult. In stepped Frank Callery, who has built up a wealth of information on b/vi welfare and life. Not only could Frank provide me with unpublished volumes of his research, but he also had disks full of modern-day images to share from three decades of editing and publishing *Insight*, the Vision Ireland magazine.

Barry Ennis was appointed Chair of Vision Sports Ireland in early 2024. He's one of the most driven and brimful-of-ideas people you'll meet. I am indebted to Barry and the Vision Sports Board of Directors, past and present, for all their support.

The staff at Vision Ireland/Vision Sports Ireland were always at hand and so helpful. Kristina Millar helped with new research and statistics. Aaron Mullaniff, CEO at Vision Sports Ireland and his

National Sports Development Manager Pádraig Healy supported me every step of the way. To the Vision Sports staff – Rosie Keogh, Sara McFadden, Sean Moyles, Sean Poland and Michael Keegan – thank you. Vision Ireland's Head Librarian Lina Kouzi gave me excellent support and drove the Vision Ireland Bookshare Ireland initiative for this book. A warm thank you also to voice-over artist Sarah Pyle. Thanks also are due to Katherine Howe at ChildVision for producing Braille copies of this book. Special thanks to my former Vision Ireland Board colleague Senator Martin Conway, who connected me with some great people.

Retired Vision Ireland CEO Des Kenny kept me on the straight and narrow with incredibly timed interventions, which ultimately found me a publisher in Michael Darcy at Martello Publishing. Michael, copy-editor Djinn von Noorden and production editor Cassia Gaden-Gilmartin at Martello are an incredibly hardworking team. Niall McCormack provided our wonderful design. Thank you also to Damien Walsh at Independent Living Movement Ireland for linking us all in.

Critical to bringing this book to you were my five test readers: Dominic Coyle, Kathleen Gleeson-Donnelly, Kevin Kelly, Michael Lavin and Neil O'Brien. You all gave me amazing and prompt constructive feedback.

Robbie Cousins was my proofreader/editor. Like so many contributors to this book, Robbie sacrificed valuable days – in his case holidays and weekends – to help me cross the line.

Securing photos for the book was made easy by so many of my contributors including Dominic Coyle, Audrey Darby, Hilary Devlin, Philip Doyle, Paul O'Rahilly, Babs Weiberg and Frank Cullinan. Thank you also to the Vision Sports team, Sportsfile and Paralympics Ireland.

There were times when writing this book where I needed to delve into the technical and ask the experts. Thank you, Ana Maia and Audrey Darby, for going that extra mile to ensure accuracy. Another shade of technical was the building of the *Out of Sight!* website. Thank you to Graham Philips, my future son in law. Also, Graham, with his fiancé, my daughter Katie, drew up initial design for the front and back covers.

I am also indebted to Helen Murphy, Prof. Michael O'Keeffe's right-hand administrator, for supporting the 'our eyes adored you' tribute.

The best part of putting this book together was meeting so many old friends and making new ones too. In some cases, we went to school together but in many cases, we crossed tracks through sport. We had some crack chatting about the glory days as well as where we're at now and hope to be in the future. The on-record chats were so beautiful and warm. The off-record chats? Sure, I couldn't be telling you those stories!

Before drawing up the list of sixty or so interviewees I chatted with Jason Smyth and Catherine Walsh. Both gave me the green light to go for this book. As I progressed so many gave me the encouragement to continue. Special mention here for Ann Cusack, owner of the Granville Hotel in Waterford and to our '96 golden girl Bridie Lynch.

Family members tell me they'll skip the book and wait for Netflix! To you my children and your partners, thanks for the patience (and all your support). Grainne, my wife, must be exhausted listening to my regular rants. For never walking away: thank you, Grainne.

It's all over now.

Your contacts: support organisations for blind and vision-impaired people in Ireland

Vision Sports Ireland
Promoting sport and physical activity for people who are blind/vision impaired of all ages and abilities.
Address: 45a Whitworth Road, Dublin, D09 RP70
Phone: +35314056030
Web: visionsports.ie

Angel Eyes NI
Parent-led charity that supports and advocates for blind and partially sighted children throughout Northern Ireland.
Address: 385 Springfield Road, Belfast
Telephone: +44 7775 873 072
Web: angeleyesni.org

British Blind Sport
British Blind Sport aim to ensure that sport and leisure facilities are accessible to every blind or partially sighted person in the UK, with the intention of improving their physical health and self-esteem.
Address: 19 Coventry Road Cubbington,
   Leamington Spa, CV32 7JN
Telephone: +44 1926 424247
Web: britishblindsport.org.uk

ChildVision
Ireland's only dedicated centre for sight-loss children, offering education, therapy and support to families.
Address: Gracepark Road, Dublin, D09 WKOH
Telephone: +353 1 8373 635
Web: childvision.ie

Féach
A parent-led Republic of Ireland charity that connects, informs and empowers parents to support their blind and vision-impaired children to ensure they thrive and lead independent lives.
Email: info@feach.ie
Web: feach.ie

Fighting Blindness
A patient-led charity that funds vision research and provides services for people with visual impairment. Their goal is to cure, support and empower.
Address: 3rd Floor, 7 Ely Place, Dublin, D02 TW98
Telephone: +353 1 6789 004
Web: fightingblindness.ie

Irish Guide Dogs for the Blind
Ireland's national charity providing guide dogs to those who are vision impaired and assistance dogs to the families of children with autism.
Address: Model Farm Road, Cork, T12 WT4A
Phone: +353 21 4878200
Web: guidedogs.ie

National League of the Blind of Ireland
Blind and vision-impaired people supporting each other towards an Ireland where people who are blind and vision impaired are full and equal members of society and are consulted on all decisions related to the services they use.
Address: 21 Hill Street, Dublin, D01 T338
Phone: +353 1 8742 792
Web: leagueoftheblind.org

RNIB NI
The Northern Ireland arm of the London-based Royal National Institute for the Blind. RNIB NI is a leading sight loss charity that provides information, support and advice.
Address: Victoria House, 15–17 Gloucester Street, Belfast, BT1 4LS
Phone +44 28 9032 9373.
Web: rnib.org.uk

Vision Ireland
Aims to enable people who are blind and vision impaired to overcome the barriers that impede their independence and participation in society.
Address: 45a Whitworth Road, Dublin, D09 RP70
Infoline: 1800 911 250
Web: vi.ie